MEDICINE

Official OET Practice Book 1

© Copyright Cambridge Boxhill Language Assessment.

This work is copyright. Apart from any use permitted under *the Copyright Act 1968*, no part may be reproduced by any process without prior written permission from Cambridge Boxhill Language Assessment.

For information in regards to OET visit the OET website:
www.occupationalenglishtest.org

First edition published May 2018

MEDICINE

Contents

An Overview of OET		1
How the test is scored		4
Test taker's guide to OET		5
	Listening	5
	Reading	7
	Writing	10
	Speaking	11
PRACTICE TEST ONE		13
	Listening (Parts A, B and C)	15
	Reading (Parts A, B and C)	25
	Writing	47
	Speaking	54
Answer keys:	Listening (Parts A, B and C)	57
	Listening (Audio script)	60
	Reading (Parts A, B and C)	70
	Writing sample response	74
PRACTICE TEST TWO		75
	Listening (Parts A, B and C)	77
	Reading (Parts A, B and C)	88
	Writing	111
	Speaking	118
Answer keys:	Listening (Parts A, B and C)	121
	Listening (Audio script)	124
	Reading (Parts A, B and C)	135
	Writing sample response	139

PRACTICE TEST THREE		**141**
	Listening (Parts A, B and C)	143
	Reading (Parts A, B and C)	153
	Writing	175
	Speaking	182
Answer keys:	Listening (Parts A, B and C)	185
	Listening (Audio script)	188
	Reading (Parts A, B and C)	198
	Writing sample response	202
How we assess Writing		**204**
How we assess Speaking		**207**
Useful language		**222**

MEDICINE

An overview of OET

About OET

OET is an international English language test that assesses the language proficiency of healthcare professionals seeking to register and practise in an English-speaking environment. It provides a validated, reliable assessment of all four language skills – listening, reading, writing and speaking – with the emphasis on communication in healthcare professional settings.

OET tests candidates from the following 12 health professions: Dentistry, Dietetics, Medicine, Nursing, Occupational Therapy, Optometry, Pharmacy, Physiotherapy, Podiatry, Radiography, Speech Pathology and Veterinary Science.

Candidates are encouraged to prepare thoroughly for their OET test.

Language proficiency and test taking skills

For more information about OET including the latest test dates and a complete list of test locations and preparation providers, as well as access to our free test preparation package Start for Success, visit the OET website: **www.occupationalenglishtest.org**

About the test

OET assesses listening, reading, writing and speaking.

There is a separate sub-test for each skill area. The Listening and Reading sub-tests are designed to assess the ability to understand spoken and written English in contexts related to general health and medicine. The sub-tests for Listening and Reading are common to all professions.

The Writing and Speaking sub-tests are specific to each profession and are designed to assess the ability to use English appropriately in the relevant professional context.

Sub-test (duration)	Content	Shows candidates can:
Listening (45 minutes)	3 tasks Common to all 12 professions	follow and understand a range of health-related spoken materials such as patient consultations and lectures.
Reading (60 minutes)	3 tasks Common to all 12 professions	read and understand different types of text on health-related subjects.
Writing (45 minutes)	1 task Specific to each profession	write a letter in a clear and accurate way which is relevant for the reader.
Speaking (20 minutes)	2 tasks Specific to each profession	effectively communicate in a real-life context through the use of role plays.

Listening sub-test

The Listening sub-test consists of three parts, and a total of 42 question items. You will hear each recording once and are expected to write your answers while listening. All three parts take 45 minutes to complete. The Listening sub-test has the following structure:

Part A – consultation extracts

Part A assesses your ability to identify specific information during a consultation. You will listen to two five-minute health professional-patient consultations and you will complete the health professional's notes using the information you hear.

Part B – short workplace extracts

Part B assesses your ability to identify the detail, gist, opinion or purpose of short extracts from the healthcare workplace. You will listen to six one-minute extracts (e.g. team briefings, handovers, or health professional-patient dialogues) and you will answer one multiple-choice question for each extract.

Part C – presentation extracts

Part C assesses your ability to follow a recorded presentation or interview on a range of accessible healthcare topics. You will listen to two different five-minute extracts and you will answer six multiple-choice questions for each extract.

Reading sub-test

The Reading sub-test consists of three parts, with a total of 42 question items. You are given 60 minutes to complete all three parts (15 minutes for Part A and 45 minutes for Part B and Part C). The Reading sub-test has the following structure:

Part A – expeditious reading task

Part A assesses your ability to locate specific information from four short texts in a quick and efficient manner. The four short texts relate to a single healthcare topic, and you must answer 20 questions in the allocated time period. The 20 questions consist of matching, sentence completion and short answer questions.

Part B and Part C – careful reading tasks

Part B assesses your ability to identify the detail, gist or purpose of six short texts sourced from the healthcare workplace (100-150 words each). The texts might consist of extracts from policy documents, hospital guidelines, manuals or internal communications, such as email or memos. For each text, there is one three-option multiple-choice question.

Part C assesses your ability to identify detailed meaning and opinion in two texts on a topic of interest to healthcare professionals (800 words each). For each text, you must answer eight four-option multiple choice questions.

www.occupationalenglishtest.org

Writing sub-test

The Writing sub-test consists of one profession specific task based on a typical workplace situation. The writing test takes 45 minutes to complete - 40 minutes to write your letter and 5 minutes at the start to read the case notes on which to base you writing. The Writing sub-test has the following structure:

The task is to write a letter, usually a referral letter but sometimes a different type of letter such as a letter of transfer or discharge.

Along with the task instructions, you will receive stimulus material (case notes and/or other related documentation) which includes information to use in your response.

Speaking sub-test

The Speaking sub-test consists of two profession specific role-plays and is delivered individually. It takes around 20 minutes to complete. In each role-play, you take your professional role (for example, as a nurse or as a pharmacist) while the interlocutor plays a patient, a client, or a patient's relative or carer. For veterinary science, the interlocutor is the owner or carer of the animal. The Speaking sub-test has the following structure:

In each Speaking test, your identity and profession are checked by the interlocutor and there is a short warm-up conversation about your professional background. Then the role-plays are introduced one by one and you have 3 minutes to prepare for each. The role-plays take about five minutes each.

You receive information for each role-play on a card that you keep while you do the role-play. The card explains the situation and what you are required to do. You may write notes on the card if you want. If you have any questions about the content of the role-play or how a role-play works, you can ask them during the preparation time.

The role-plays are based on typical workplace situations and reflect the demands made on a health professional in those situations. The interlocutor follows a script so that the Speaking test structure is similar for each candidate. The interlocutor also has detailed information to use in each role-play. Different role-plays are used for different candidates at the same test administration.

How the test is scored

You will receive your results in the form of a score on a scale from 0 to 500 for each of the four sub-tests:

OET Results table

OET results to August 2018	OET score from September 2018	OET band descriptors	IELTS equivalent band score
A	500 490 480 470 460 450	Can communicate very fluently and effectively with patients and health professionals using appropriate register, tone and lexis. Shows complete understanding of any kind of written or spoken language.	8.0 - 9.0
B	440 430 420 410 400 390 380 370 360 350	Can communicate effectively with patients and health professionals using appropriate register, tone and lexis, with only occasional inaccuracies and hesitations. Shows good understanding in a range of clinical contexts.	7.0 – 7.5
C+	340 330 320 310 300		6.5
C	290 280 270 260 250 240 230 220 210 200	Can maintain the interaction in a relevant healthcare environment despite occasional errors and lapses, and follow standard spoken language normally encountered in his/her field of specialisation.	5.5 – 6.0
D	190 180 170 160 150 140 130 120 110 100	Can maintain some interaction and understand straightforward factual information in his/her field of specialisation, but may ask for clarification. Frequent errors, inaccuracies and mis-or overuse of technical language can cause strain in communication.	Less than 5.5
E	90 80 70 60 50 40 30 20 10 0	Can manage simple interaction on familiar topics and understand the main point in short, simple messages, provided he/she can ask for clarification. High density of errors and mis- or overuse of technical language can cause significant strain and breakdowns in communication.	

Test taker's guide to OET

Listening

Part A

Remember, in **Part A** you listen to a recording of 2 consultations between a health professional and a patient (dialogue). You take notes while you listen. This part of the test usually lasts around 15 minutes. Before you attempt the Practice Test, consider some important tips below.

Do

- Use the sub-headings to guide you .
- Give specific rather than general information from the recording.

Don't

- Jump ahead or back: the gaps follow the sequence of the recording.
- Write full sentences: a word or short phrase is sufficient.
- Don't waste valuable time using an eraser to correct a mistake if you make one. Simply cross out any words you don't want the person marking your paper to accept; this takes a lot less time and you will not be penalised.

Part B

Remember, in **Part B** you listen to six recorded extracts from the healthcare workplace. You answer one multiple-choice question for each extract. This part of the test usually lasts around 10 minutes.

Do

- Read the contextual information for each extract to understand the interaction you will hear.
- Read through each question carefully.
- Mark your answers on this Question Paper by filling in the circle using a 2B pencil.

Don't

- Select your answer until you have heard the whole extract.
- Fill in more than one circle on the Question Paper as the scanner will not be able to recognise your answer and you will not receive any marks for that question.

Part C

Remember, in **Part C** you listen to 2 recordings of a recorded presentation or interview on a health-related issue. You will answer six multiple-choice questions for each recording while you listen. This part of the test usually lasts around 15 minutes. Before you attempt the Practice Test, consider some important tips below.

Do

- Read through each question carefully.
- Mark your answers on this Question Paper by filling in the circle using a 2B pencil.

Don't

- Wait for key words in the question or answer options to be said in the recording. The speaker(s) will often use synonyms of the words you read.
- Fill in more than one circle on the Question Paper as the scanner will not be able to recognise your answer and you will not receive any marks for that question.

General

- Have a spare pen or pencil ready just in case.
- Stay relaxed and receptive – ready to listen.
- Focus on listening and understanding then recording your answer.
- Demonstrate that you have understood the recording (as well as heard it).
- Take a sample test under test conditions beforehand so you know what it feels like.
- Don't be distracted by what is going on around you (e.g., sneezing, a nervous candidate at the next desk)
- When the recording starts, use the time allowed to look through the questions carefully, scanning the headings and questions so you know what to listen out for.
- Use common abbreviations and symbols.
- Write clearly; don't make it difficult for the assessor to read your responses as you may not get all the marks you could.
- Don't lose your place during the test; remain focused on each question.

Checking at the end

- Think twice about going back to change something – it may be better to leave what you wrote the first time if you are not sure.
- Don't leave any blanks; have a guess at the answer.

Developing your listening skills

- You should practise listening to English delivered at natural speed in a variety of voices and contexts. Learners who do this regularly are more confident at extracting key information and gist meaning, even when they are not able to decode every single word or phrase. Make sure you are exposed to speakers of different ages and backgrounds, and to the language of different contexts (e.g., informal discussions, formal lectures, etc.).
- Although it is useful to practise exam techniques by using exam materials and course books, you should also use real-life sources to develop your listening skills. You can find a variety of authentic sources for free on the internet, particularly in the form of training videos and professional development talks.
- Practise dealing with listening texts in a variety of ways. For example, you can listen to a text once for the gist, and produce a summary of the main ideas or attitudes expressed by the speakers. You can then listen to the same text a second time in order to retrieve specific information or to focus on useful language.
- At a high level in OET Listening, it is not enough to be able to pick out particular words or specific details. You need to be able to understand the overall meaning of what the speakers are saying. It is important to practise following a speaker's line of argument and identifying his/her opinion or attitude.

What to expect in the test

- The instructions for each task are given on the question paper, and you will also hear them on the recording. They give you information about the topic and the speakers, and tell you about the type of task you have to do.
- There is a pause before each section to give you time to read through and think about the questions. Use the time to familiarise yourself with the task and start to predict what you are likely to hear.
- Use the task on the paper to guide you through the recording as you answer the questions.

MEDICINE

Reading

Part A

Remember, in **Part A** you locate specific information from four short texts related to a single healthcare topic. You have 15 minutes to answer 20 questions. Before you attempt the Practice Test, consider some important tips below.

Do

» Keep the Text Booklet open in front of you so that you can see all the texts and the answer booklet at the same time. You need to be able to move between the different texts quickly and easily.

» Use the headings and layout of the short texts to get a quick initial idea of the type of information they contain and how they are organised. This will help you select which text you need for each section of the test.

» For short answer and sentence completion questions, use the statement to find out what type of information you need and decide which of the short texts is likely to contain that information. Then navigate to the relevant part of the text.

» Use correct spelling: incorrectly spelt answers do not receive any marks. You may use either British or American spelling variations (e.g. anemia and anaemia are both acceptable).

Don't

» The answers for Part A need to be consistent with the information of the texts. It is not a good strategy to use your professional background knowledge to answer Part A and avoid skimming and scanning the text.

» Use words with similar meaning to words in the texts. These words are known as synonyms.

» Waste valuable time using an eraser to correct a mistake if you make one. You may, for example, accidentally include an extra word or write the wrong word in the wrong space. Simply cross out any words you don't want the assessor marking your paper to accept; this takes a lot less time and you will not be penalised.

» Begin Part A by simply reading all texts from beginning to end as this will waste valuable time. Use the questions to guide you to which text to read first.

Part B

Remember, in **Part B** you answer one multiple-choice question about six short texts sourced from the healthcare workplace. The combined time for Parts B and C is 45 minutes. Before you attempt the Practice Test, consider some important tips below.

Do

» Read the contextual information for each text to help you understand the purpose and audience of the content.

» Read each answer option carefully and scan the text for evidence to support this option being correct or incorrect.

» Manage your time carefully. You should aim to spend the majority of the 45 minutes on Part C.

» Mark your answers on this Question Paper by filling in the circle using a 2B pencil.

Don't

» Read each text before reading the questions. You need to be efficient with your time: read the answer options and then focus on the text.

» Be distracted by unfamiliar vocabulary. Use the surrounding words to approximate the meaning and continue to search for the answer. Questions can often be answered without understanding all the vocabulary.

» Fill in more than one circle on the Question Paper as the scanner will not be able to recognise your answer and you will not receive any marks for that question.

Part C

Remember, in **Part C** you answer eight multiple-choice questions on each of two texts which are about a topic of interest to healthcare professionals. The combined time for Parts B and C is 45 minutes. Before you attempt the Practice Test, consider some important points below.

Do

- There are no thematic links between the two texts. Focus on one text at a time rather than moving backwards and forwards between them.
- Manage your time carefully. Allow enough time for both Part C texts as the reading skills it requires are quite considered and detailed.
- Read each question carefully, looking out for key words.
- Consider each of the options and explain to yourself what makes each one right or wrong.
- If you are unsure about a question, consider moving on and coming back to it later.
- Mark your answers on this Question Paper by filling in the circle using a 2B pencil.

Don't

- Get stuck on one question – keep going and come back to it at the end when you have answered all other questions. Marks are not deducted for incorrect answers.
- Fill in more than one circle on the Question Paper as the scanner will not be able to recognise your answer and you will not receive any marks for that question.

General

- Have a spare pen and pencil ready just in case.
- Bring and use a soft (2B) pencil. Remember you cannot use a pen to answer the multiple-choice questions for Parts B and C. It is a good idea to bring one or two extra 2B pencils as spares or a small pencil sharpener.
- Note how the text is organised (e.g., with sub-headings, tables/diagrams etc.).
- Write on the texts if it helps you (e.g., underlining key words and phrases etc.) but don't make it more difficult for you to read by adding too many marks.
- When checking at the end, don't make any last-minute changes unless you are sure.

Developing your reading skills

- You should practise reading a variety of text types in English so that you become familiar with a wide range of language and organisational features. Candidates who do this regularly are more confident at understanding the overall function and message of texts and at following a line of argument in a text.
- Although it is useful to practise exam techniques by using exam materials and course books, you should also use real-life sources to develop your reading skills. Following up on your own professional or personal interests is a good way to increase your exposure to different types of texts.
- Practise dealing with texts in a variety of ways. For example, you could read a text once for the gist, and produce a summary of the main ideas or attitudes expressed by the writers. You could then read the same text a second time in order to retrieve specific information or to focus on useful language.
- At a high level in OET Reading, it is not enough to be able to pick out particular words or specific details. You need to be able to understand the overall meaning of the text. It is important to practise following a writer's line of argument as well as identifying specific pieces of information.
- Take the sample test under test conditions beforehand so you know what it feels like. For Part A, set yourself a strict time limit of 15 minutes. For Part B, set your timer for 45 minutes.

MEDICINE

What to expect in the test

» The instructions for each task are given on the question paper. They give you information about the topic and the texts, and tell you about the type of task you have to do.

» You will complete the Reading sub-test in two parts. First you will be given the Text Booklet and the Answer Booklet for Part A. When the 15 minutes for Part A have finished, these will be collected from you. You will then be given the Text Booklet for Parts B & C.

» You will not be able to go back to Part A, even if you finish Parts B & C early. Leave yourself enough time in each Part to check your answers.

» You may write your answers in either **pen** or **pencil** for Part A.

Writing

Do

- » Take time to understand the task requirements.
- » Use your own words to paraphrase or summarise longer pieces of information from the case notes.
- » Make sure you understand the situation described in the case notes.
- » Think about how best to organise your letter before you start writing.
- » Use the space provided to plan your letter (though a draft is not compulsory).
- » Use the five minutes' reading time effectively to understand the task set
    - What is your role?
    - Who is your audience (the intended reader)?
    - What is the current situation?
    - How urgent is the current situation?
    - What is the main point you must communicate to the reader?
    - What supporting information is necessary to give to the reader?
    - What background information is useful to the reader?
    - What information is unnecessary for the reader? Why is it unnecessary?
- » Explain the current situation at the start of the letter (e.g., perhaps an emergency situation).
- » Use the names and address given.
- » Set out the names, address, date and other information to start the letter clearly.
- » As you write, indicate each new paragraph clearly, perhaps by leaving a blank line.

Don't

- » Include everything from the case notes – select information relevant to the task.
- » Simply copy chunks of text from the case notes.
- » Write notes or numbered points.

General

- » Have a spare pen and pencil ready, just in case.
- » Fill in the cover pages for the task booklet and the answer booklet correctly.
- » Fill in your personal information on the answer sheet correctly.
- » Take a sample test under test conditions beforehand so you know what it feels like.
- » Practise writing clearly if you have poor handwriting.
- » Write clearly and legibly.

Checking at the end

- » Make sure your letter communicates what you intend.
- » Make sure you meet the basic task requirements:
    - length of the body of the text approximately 180–200 words
    - full sentences, not note form
    - appropriate letter format.
- » Check for any simple grammar and spelling errors that you may have made.
- » If a page is messy, use clear marks (e.g., arrows, numbers) to show the sequence in which the parts of your text should be read.
- » Cross out clearly anything you do not want the assessors to read.

MEDICINE

Speaking

Do

Candidates should use the prompts/notes on the role-play card to guide them through the role-play:

- What is your role?
- What role is your interlocutor playing – patient, parent/son/daughter, carer?
- Where is the conversation taking place?
- What is the current situation?
- How urgent is the situation?
- What background information are you given about the patient and the situation?
- What are you required to do?
- What is the main purpose of the conversation (e.g., explain, find out, reassure, persuade etc.)?
- What other elements of the situation do you know about (e.g., the patient appears nervous or angry, you don't have much time etc.)?
- What information do you need to give the patient (remember, though, this is not a test of your professional skills)?

Don't

- Rely on scripted or rehearsed phrases during the test. Many of these phrases will not be appropriate for certain role-plays.
- Speak about topics not related to the role-play. Your focus should be on what's on your role-play card.

Information about role-play cards

Candidates will have an opportunity to read through the role-play card before starting each role-play. Both role-play cards are laid out in a similar way. At the top of the role-play card is information about the setting (i.e. where the conversation is taking place). Candidates receive information on each role-play card, which he/she keeps while doing the role-play. Candidates may write notes on the role-play card if they want to.

The role-play card explains the situation and what candidates are required to do. If candidates have any questions about the content of the role-play or how a role-play works, they may ask for clarification before starting.

The top paragraph contains background information about the patient and his/her situation. It will be made clear if the interlocutor is taking on the role of the patient or somebody talking on behalf of the patient (i.e., the patient's carer, parent, etc.). The bottom half of the role-play card contains information to assist candidates in what they need to mention during the role-play. Each role-play card contains approximately 100-150 words (prompts/notes to guide candidates during the role-play).

The Speaking sub-test is in three parts:

1. Warm-up conversation (this is not assessed)
» format of the test explained
» candidate helped to relax
» questions asked about areas of professional interest, previous work experience, future plans, etc.

2. First role-play (assessed)
» candidate handed role-play card
» candidate has 2-3 minutes to prepare
» candidate can ask questions to clarify before role-play starts
» role-play is conducted (approximately 5 minutes)

3. Second role-play (assessed)
» above procedure is repeated using a different role-play

Using the Speaking practice tests
» Copy the role-play.
» Ask a friend or colleague to play the role of the patient (or patient's carer, etc.).
» Take the role of the health professional.
» Ask another friend or colleague to observe the role-play and give you feedback on your performance.
» Read the information on the role-play card carefully.
» You have to deal with the case details as outlined on the role-play card by asking and answering questions put to you by the patient or client.
» Speak as naturally as possible.
» Remember it is important to be interested in the welfare of the patient and to reassure the patient or relation of the patient that the treatment being proposed is appropriate.
» Keep to the time limit of 5 minutes (approximate) for each role-play.
» Ask the friend or colleague who observed for comments and feedback.

MEDICINE

PRACTICE TEST 1

To listen to the audio, visit
https://www.occupationalenglishtest.org/audio

LISTENING SUB-TEST – QUESTION PAPER

CANDIDATE NUMBER:

LAST NAME:

FIRST NAME:

MIDDLE NAMES:

PROFESSION:

VENUE:

TEST DATE:

Candidate details and photo will be printed here.

Passport Photo

CANDIDATE DECLARATION

By signing this, you agree not to disclose or use in any way (other than to take the test) or assist any other person to disclose or use any OET test or sub-test content. If you cheat or assist in any cheating, use any unfair practice, break any of the rules or regulations, or ignore any advice or information, you may be disqualified and your results may not be issued at the sole discretion of CBLA. CBLA also reserves its right to take further disciplinary action against you and to pursue any other remedies permitted by law. If a candidate is suspected of and investigated for malpractice, their personal details and details of the investigation may be passed to a third party where required.

CANDIDATE SIGNATURE: _____

TIME: APPROXIMATELY **40 MINUTES**

INSTRUCTIONS TO CANDIDATES

DO NOT open this question paper until you are told to do so.

One mark will be granted for each correct answer.

Answer **ALL** questions. Marks are **NOT** deducted for incorrect answers.

At the end of the test, you will have two minutes to check your answers.

At the end of the test, hand in this **Question Paper**.

You must not remove OET material from the test room.

HOW TO ANSWER THE QUESTIONS

Part A: Write your answers on this **Question Paper** by filling in the blanks. **Example: Patient:** _Ray Sands_

Part B & Part C: Mark your answers on this **Question Paper** by filling in the circle using a 2B pencil. **Example:** Ⓐ Ⓑ Ⓒ

www.occupationalenglishtest.org
© Cambridge Boxhill Language Assessment – ABN 51 988 559 414
[CANDIDATE NO.] LISTENING QUESTION PAPER 01/12

Occupational English Test

Listening Test

This test has three parts. In each part you'll hear a number of different extracts. At the start of each extract, you'll hear this sound: --beep—

You'll have time to read the questions before you hear each extract and you'll hear each extract **ONCE ONLY**. Complete your answers as you listen.

At the end of the test you'll have two minutes to check your answers.

Part A

In this part of the test, you'll hear two different extracts. In each extract, a health professional is talking to a patient.

For **questions 1-24**, complete the notes with information you hear.

Now, look at the notes for extract one.

Extract 1: Questions 1-12

You hear an obstetrician talking to a patient called Melissa Gordon. For **questions 1-12**, complete the notes with a word or short phrase.

You now have 30 seconds to look at the notes.

Patient	Melissa Gordon
	• works as a **(1)**
Medical history	• has occasional **(2)**
	• is allergic to **(3)**
	• has a **(4)** _____ diet
	• non-smoker
	• this will be her second child
	• needed **(5)** _____ treatment before first pregnancy
	• first baby presented as **(6)** _____
	- **(7)** _____ required during intervention
	• after giving birth, had problems with **(8)**
	- helped by midwife
Baby's father	• family history of **(9)** _____
	• child from previous marriage has **(10)** _____
Points raised	• not keen on amniocentesis
	• enquired about the possibility of **(11)** _____ testing
	• provided her with a leaflet on preparing **(12)** _____ for new baby

Extract 2: Questions 13-24

You hear a GP talking to a new patient called Mike Royce. For **questions 13-24**, complete the notes with a word or short phrase.

You now have thirty seconds to look at the notes.

Patient Mike Royce

New patient transferring from another practice

Description of initial symptoms

- severe left knee pain in **(13)** _____ area
- worsened after an accident at work
- developed **(14)** _____ on back of knee (described as trigger points.)

Impact on daily life

- unable to **(15)** _____ while working (house painter)
- problems climbing ladders

Initial treatment

- exercise programme including
    - stretching exercises
    - rest
- **(16)** _____ for pain

Developments in condition

- GP suspected **(17)** _____
- prescribed hospital-based rehabilitation
- temporary improvement noted

Current condition

- muscular problem diagnosed by **(18)** _____
  - was performing treatment on **(19)** _____
- experiencing insomnia and **(20)** _____
- suspects **(21)** _____ (own research)
- has recorded experiences in **(22)** _____
- beginning to experience pain in both **(23)** _____

Suggested course of action

- recommend referral to **(24)** _____

That is the end of Part A. Now look at Part B.

Part B

In this part of the test, you'll hear six different extracts. In each extract, you'll hear people talking in a different healthcare setting.

For **questions 25-30**, choose the answer (**A**, **B** or **C**) which fits best according to what you hear. You'll have time to read each question before you listen. Complete your answers as you listen.

Now look at question 25.

25. You hear a dietitian talking to a patient.

What is she doing?

- **A** correcting the patient's misconception about obesity
- **B** describing the link between obesity and other diseases
- **C** stressing the need for a positive strategy aimed at weight loss

26. You hear members of a hospital committee discussing problems in the X-ray department.

The problems are due to a delay in

- **A** buying a replacement machine.
- **B** getting approval for a repair to a machine.
- **C** identifying a problem with a particular machine.

27. You hear a senior nurse giving feedback to a trainee after a training exercise.

The trainee accepts that he failed to

- **A** locate the CPR board quickly enough.
- **B** deal with the CPR board on his own.
- **C** install the CPR board correctly.

20 PRACTICE TEST **1**

28. You hear a trainee nurse asking his senior colleague about the use of anti-embolism socks (AES) for a patient.

The patient isn't wearing the socks because

- A she's suffering from arterial disease in her legs.
- B there is sensory loss in her legs.
- C her legs are too swollen.

29. You hear a vet talking about her involvement in the management of the practice where she works.

How does she feel about her role?

- A She accepts that it's become surprisingly complex.
- B She wishes her boss took more interest in the finances.
- C She values the greater understanding it gives her of her work.

30. You hear a physiotherapist giving a presentation about a study she's been involved in.

She suggests that her findings are of particular interest because of

- A the age of the subjects.
- B the type of disorder involved.
- C the length of time covered by the study.

That is the end of Part B. Now look at Part C.

Part C

In this part of the test, you'll hear two different extracts. In each extract, you'll hear health professionals talking about aspects of their work.

For **questions 31-42**, choose the answer (**A, B** or **C**) which fits best according to what you hear. Complete your answers as you listen.

Now look at extract one.

Extract 1: Questions 31-36

You hear a sports physiotherapist called Chris Maloney giving a presentation in which he describes treating a high jumper with a knee injury.

You now have 90 seconds to read **questions 31-36**.

31. When Chris first met the patient, he found out that

    A   she was considering retirement from her sport.

    B   her state of mind had aggravated the pain in her knee.

    C   she had ignored professional advice previously offered to her.

32. During his assessment of the patient's knee, Chris decided that

    A   her body type wasn't naturally suited to her sport.

    B   the pain she felt was mainly located in one place.

    C   some key muscles weren't strong enough.

33. In the first stage of his treatment, Chris

    A   was careful to explain his methods in detail.

    B   soon discovered what was causing the problem.

    C   used evidence from MRI scans to inform his approach.

34. Why did Chris decide against the practice known as 'taping'?

    A   The patient was reluctant to use it.

    B   It might give a false sense of security.

    C   The treatment was succeeding without it.

35. In the patient's gym work, Chris's main concern was to ensure that she

   A   tried out a wide range of fitness exercises.

   B   focussed on applying the correct techniques.

   C   was capable of managing her own training regime.

36. Why was the patient's run-up technique changed?

   A   to enable her to gain more speed before take off

   B   to reduce the stress placed on her take-off leg

   C   to reinforce the break from her old mindset

Now look at extract two.

Extract 2: Questions 37-42

You hear a clinical psychiatrist called Dr Anthony Gibbens giving a presentation about the value of individual patients' experiences and 'stories' in medicine.

You now have 90 seconds to read **questions 37-42**.

37. What impressed Dr Gibbens about the case study that was sent to him?

   A   where it was originally published

   B   how controversial its contents were

   C   his colleague's reasons for sending it to him

38. Dr Gibbens has noticed that people who read his books

   A   gain insights into their mental health problems.

   B   see an improvement in personal relationships.

   C   benefit from a subtle change in behaviour.

39. What disadvantage of doctors using patients' stories does Dr Gibbens identify?

- A evidence-based research being disregarded
- B patients being encouraged to self-diagnose
- C a tendency to jump to conclusions

40. In Dr Gibbens' opinion, why should patients' stories inform medical practice?

- A They provide an insight not gained from numbers alone.
- B They prove useful when testing new theories.
- C They are more accessible than statistics.

41. How does Dr Gibbens feel about randomised medical trials?

- A He questions the reliability of the method.
- B He is suspicious of the way data are selected for them.
- C He is doubtful of their value when used independently.

42. When talking about the use of narratives in medicine in the future, Dr Gibbens reveals

- A his determination that they should be used to inform research.
- B his commitment to making them more widely accepted.
- C his optimism that they will be published more widely.

That is the end of Part C.

You now have two minutes to check your answers.

END OF THE LISTENING TEST

READING SUB-TEST – TEXT BOOKLET: PART A

CANDIDATE NUMBER:
LAST NAME:
FIRST NAME:
MIDDLE NAMES:
PROFESSION:
VENUE:
TEST DATE:

Candidate details and photo will be printed here.

Passport Photo

CANDIDATE DECLARATION
By signing this, you agree not to disclose or use in any way (other than to take the test) or assist any other person to disclose or use any OET test or sub-test content. If you cheat or assist in any cheating, use any unfair practice, break any of the rules or regulations, or ignore any advice or information, you may be disqualified and your results may not be issued at the sole discretion of CBLA. CBLA also reserves its right to take further disciplinary action against you and to pursue any other remedies permitted by law. If a candidate is suspected of and investigated for malpractice, their personal details and details of the investigation may be passed to a third party where required.

CANDIDATE SIGNATURE: _____

INSTRUCTIONS TO CANDIDATES

You must **NOT** remove OET material from the test room.

www.occupationalenglishtest.org
© Cambridge Boxhill Language Assessment – ABN 51 988 559 414

The use of feeding tubes in paediatrics: Texts

Text A

Paediatric nasogastric tube use

Nasogastric is the most common route for enteral feeding. It is particularly useful in the short term, and when it is necessary to avoid a surgical procedure to insert a gastrostomy device. However, in the long term, gastrostomy feeding may be more suitable.

Issues associated with paediatric nasogastric tube feeding include:

- The procedure for inserting the tube is traumatic for the majority of children.
- The tube is very noticeable.
- Patients are likely to pull out the tube making regular re-insertion necessary.
- Aspiration, if the tube is incorrectly placed.
- Increased risk of gastro-esophageal reflux with prolonged use.
- Damage to the skin on the face.

Text B

Inserting the nasogastric tube

All tubes must be radio opaque throughout their length and have externally visible markings.

1. Wide bore:
    - for short-term use only.
    - should be changed every seven days.
    - range of sizes for paediatric use is 6 Fr to 10 Fr.

2. Fine bore:
    - for long-term use.
    - should be changed every 30 days.

In general, tube sizes of 6 Fr are used for standard feeds, and 7-10 Fr for higher density and fibre feeds. Tubes come in a range of lengths, usually 55cm, 75cm or 85cm.

Wash and dry hands thoroughly. Place all the equipment needed on a clean tray.

- Find the most appropriate position for the child, depending on age and/or ability to co-operate. Older children may be able to sit upright with head support. Younger children may sit on a parent's lap. Infants may be wrapped in a sheet or blanket.
- Check the tube is intact then stretch it to remove any shape retained from being packaged.
- Measure from the tip of the nose to the bottom of the ear lobe, then from the ear lobe to xiphisternum. The length of tube can be marked with indelible pen or a note taken of the measurement marks on the tube (for neonates: measure from the nose to ear and then to the halfway point between xiphisternum and umbilicus).
- Lubricate the end of the tube using a water-based lubricant.
- Gently pass the tube into the child's nostril, advancing it along the floor of the nasopharynx to the oropharynx. Ask the child to swallow a little water, or offer a younger child their soother, to assist passage of the tube down the oesophagus. Never advance the tube against resistance.
- If the child shows signs of breathlessness or severe coughing, remove the tube immediately.
- Lightly secure the tube with tape until the position has been checked.

Text C

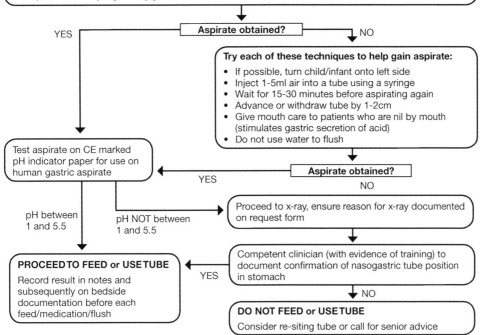

A pH of between 1 and 5.5 is reliable confirmation that the tube is not in the lung, however, it does not confirm gastric placement. If this is any concern, the patient should proceed to x-ray in order to confirm tube position.

Where pH readings fall between 5 and 6 it is recommended that a second competent person checks the reading or retests.

Text D

Administering feeds/fluid via a feeding tube

Feeds are ordered through a referral to the dietitian.

When feeding directly into the small bowel, feeds must be delivered continuously via a feeding pump. The small bowel cannot hold large volumes of feed.

Feed bottles must be changed every six hours, or every four hours for expressed breast milk.

Under no circumstances should the feed be decanted from the container in which it is sent up from the special feeds unit.

All feeds should be monitored and recorded hourly using a fluid balance chart.

If oral feeding is appropriate, this must also be recorded.

The child should be measured and weighed before feeding commences and then twice weekly.

The use of this feeding method should be re-assessed, evaluated and recorded daily.

END OF PART A
THIS TEXT BOOKLET WILL BE COLLECTED

READING SUB-TEST – QUESTION PAPER: PART A

CANDIDATE NUMBER:

LAST NAME:

FIRST NAME:

MIDDLE NAMES:

PROFESSION:

VENUE:

TEST DATE:

Candidate details and photo will be printed here.

Passport Photo

CANDIDATE DECLARATION

By signing this, you agree not to disclose or use in any way (other than to take the test) or assist any other person to disclose or use any OET test or sub-test content. If you cheat or assist in any cheating, use any unfair practice, break any of the rules or regulations, or ignore any advice or information, you may be disqualified and your results may not be issued at the sole discretion of CBLA. CBLA also reserves its right to take further disciplinary action against you and to pursue any other remedies permitted by law. If a candidate is suspected of and investigated for malpractice, their personal details and details of the investigation may be passed to a third party where required.

CANDIDATE SIGNATURE: _____

TIME: 15 MINUTES

INSTRUCTIONS TO CANDIDATES

DO NOT open this **Question Paper** or the **Text Booklet** until you are told to do so.

Write your answers on the spaces provided on this **Question Paper.**

You must answer the questions within the 15-minute time limit.

One mark will be granted for each correct answer.

Answer **ALL** questions. Marks are **NOT** deducted for incorrect answers.

At the end of the 15 minutes, hand in this **Question Paper** and the **Text Booklet.**

DO NOT remove OET material from the test room.

www.occupationalenglishtest.org
© Cambridge Boxhill Language Assessment – ABN 51 988 559 414

[CANDIDATE NO.] READING QUESTION PAPER PART A 01/04

Part A

TIME: 15 minutes

- Look at the four texts, **A-D**, in the separate **Text Booklet**.
- For each question, **1-20**, look through the texts, **A-D**, to find the relevant information.
- Write your answers on the spaces provided in this **Question Paper**.
- Answer all the questions within the 15-minute time limit.
- Your answers should be correctly spelt.

The use of feeding tubes in paediatrics: Questions

Questions 1-7

For each question, **1-7**, decide which text (**A**, **B**, **C** or **D**) the information comes from.
You may use any letter more than once.

In which text can you find information about

1   the risks of feeding a child via a nasogastric tube? _____

2   calculating the length of tube that will be required for a patient? _____

3   when alternative forms of feeding may be more appropriate than nasogastric? _____

4   who to consult over a patient's liquid food requirements? _____

5   the outward appearance of the tubes? _____

6   knowing when it is safe to go ahead with the use of a tube for feeding? _____

7   how regularly different kinds of tubes need replacing? _____

Questions 8-15

Answer each of the questions, **8-15**, with a word or short phrase from one of the texts. Each answer may include words, numbers or both.

8 What type of tube should you use for patients who need nasogastric feeding for an

 extended period?

 _____

9 What should you apply to a feeding tube to make it easier to insert?

 _____

10 What should you use to keep the tube in place temporarily?

 _____

11 What equipment should you use initially to aspirate a feeding tube?

 _____

12 If initial aspiration of the feeding tube is unsuccessful, how long should you wait before trying again?

 _____

13 How should you position a patient during a second attempt to obtain aspirate?

 _____

14 If aspirate exceeds pH 5.5, where should you take the patient to confirm the position of the tube?

 _____

15 What device allows for the delivery of feeds via the small bowel?

 _____

Questions 16-20

Complete each of the sentences, **16-20**, with a word or short phrase from one of the texts. Each answer may include words, numbers or both.

16 If a feeding tube isn't straight when you unwrap it, you should _____ it.

17 Patients are more likely to experience _____ if they need long-term feeding via a tube.

18 If you need to give the patient a standard liquid feed, the tube to use is _____ in size.

19 You must take out the feeding tube at once if the patient is coughing badly or is experiencing _____ .

20 If a child is receiving _____ via a feeding tube, you should replace the feed bottle after four hours.

END OF PART A

THIS QUESTION PAPER WILL BE COLLECTED

READING SUB-TEST – QUESTION PAPER: PARTS B & C

CANDIDATE NUMBER:

LAST NAME:

FIRST NAME:

MIDDLE NAMES:

PROFESSION:

VENUE:

TEST DATE:

Candidate details and photo will be printed here.

Passport Photo

CANDIDATE DECLARATION
By signing this, you agree not to disclose or use in any way (other than to take the test) or assist any other person to disclose or use any OET test or sub-test content. If you cheat or assist in any cheating, use any unfair practice, break any of the rules or regulations, or ignore any advice or information, you may be disqualified and your results may not be issued at the sole discretion of CBLA. CBLA also reserves its right to take further disciplinary action against you and to pursue any other remedies permitted by law. If a candidate is suspected of and investigated for malpractice, their personal details and details of the investigation may be passed to a third party where required.

CANDIDATE SIGNATURE: _____

TIME: 45 MINUTES

INSTRUCTIONS TO CANDIDATES

DO NOT open this **Question Paper** until you are told to do so.

One mark will be granted for each correct answer.

Answer **ALL** questions. Marks are **NOT** deducted for incorrect answers.

At the end of the test, hand in this **Question Paper**.

HOW TO ANSWER THE QUESTIONS:

Mark your answers on this **Question Paper** by filling in the circle using a 2B pencil. **Example:** Ⓐ Ⓑ Ⓒ

www.occupationalenglishtest.org
© Cambridge Boxhill Language Assessment – ABN 51 988 559 414
[CANDIDATE NO.] READING QUESTION PAPER PARTS B & C 01/16

Part B

In this part of the test, there are six short extracts relating to the work of health professionals. For **questions 1-6**, choose answer (**A**, **B** or **C**) which you think fits best according to the text.

1. If vaccines have been stored incorrectly,

    A   this should be reported.

    B   staff should dispose of them securely.

    C   they should be sent back to the supplier.

Manual extract: effective cold chain
The cold chain is the system of transporting and storing vaccines within the temperature range of +2°C to +8°C from the place of manufacture to the point of administration. Maintenance of the cold chain is essential for maintaining vaccine potency and, in turn, vaccine effectiveness.
Purpose-built vaccine refrigerators (PBVR) are the preferred means of storage for vaccines. Domestic refrigerators are not designed for the special temperature needs of vaccine storage.
Despite best practices, cold chain breaches sometimes occur. Do not discard or use any vaccines exposed to temperatures below +2°C or above +8°C without obtaining further advice. Isolate vaccines and contact the state or territory public health bodies for advice on the National Immunisation Program vaccines and the manufacturer for privately purchased vaccines.

2. According to the extract, prior to making a home visit, nurses must

- (A) record the time they leave the practice.
- (B) refill their bag with necessary items.
- (C) communicate their intentions to others.

Nurse home visit guidelines

When the nurse is ready to depart, he/she must advise a minimum of two staff members that he/she is commencing home visits, with one staff member responsible for logging the nurse's movements. More than one person must be made aware of the nurse's movements; failure to do so could result in the breakdown of communication and increased risk to the nurse and/or practice.

On return to the practice, the nurse will immediately advise staff members of his/her return. This time will be documented on the patient visit list, and then scanned and filed by administration staff. The nurse will then attend to any specimens, cold chain requirements, restocking of the nurse kit and biohazardous waste.

3. What is being described in this section of the guidelines?

- (A) changes in procedures
- (B) best practice procedures
- (C) exceptions to the procedures

Guidelines for dealing with hospital waste
All biological waste must be carefully stored and disposed of safely. Contaminated materials such as blood bags, dirty dressings and disposable needles are also potentially hazardous and must be treated accordingly. If biological waste and contaminated materials are not disposed of properly, staff and members of the community could be exposed to infectious material and become infected. It is essential for the hospital to have protocols for dealing with biological waste and contaminated materials. All staff must be familiar with them and follow them.
The disposal of biohazardous materials is time-consuming and expensive, so it is important to separate out non-contaminated waste such as paper, packaging and non-sterile materials. Make separate disposal containers available where waste is created so that staff can sort the waste as it is being discarded.

4. When is it acceptable for a health professional to pass on confidential information given by a patient?

   A if non-disclosure could adversely affect those involved

   B if the patient's treatment might otherwise be compromised

   C if the health professional would otherwise be breaking the law

Extract from guidelines: Patient Confidentiality
Where a patient objects to information being shared with other health professionals involved in their care, you should explain how disclosure would benefit the continuity and quality of care. If their decision has implications for the proposed treatment, it will be necessary to inform the patient of this. Ultimately if they refuse, you must respect their decision, even if it means that for reasons of safety you must limit your treatment options. You should record their decision within their clinical notes.
It may be in the public interest to disclose information received in confidence without consent, for example, information about a serious crime. It is important that confidentiality may only be broken in this way in exceptional circumstances and then only after careful consideration. This means you can justify your actions and point out the possible harm to the patient or other interested parties if you hadn't disclosed the information. Theft, fraud or damage to property would generally not warrant a breach of confidence.

5. The purpose of the email to practitioners about infection control obligations is to

   (A) act as a reminder of their obligations.

   (B) respond to a specific query they have raised.

   (C) announce a change in regulations affecting them.

Email from Dental Board of Australia
Dear Practitioner,
You may be aware of the recent media and public interest in standards of infection control in dental practice. As regulators of the profession, we are concerned that there has been doubt among registered dental practitioners about these essential standards.
Registered dental practitioners must comply with the National Board's Guidelines on infection control. The guidelines list the reference material that you must have access to and comply with, including the National Health and Medical Research Council's (NHMRC) Guidelines for the prevention and control of infection in healthcare.
We believe that most dental practitioners consistently comply with these guidelines and implement appropriate infection control protocols. However, the consequences for non-compliance with appropriate infection control measures will be significant for you and also for your patients and the community.

6. The results of the study described in the memo may explain why

   (A) superior communication skills may protect women from dementia.

   (B) female dementia sufferers have better verbal skills.

   (C) mild dementia in women can remain undiagnosed.

Memo to staff: Women and Dementia
Please read this extract from a recent research paper
Women's superior verbal skills could work against them when it comes to recognizing Alzheimer's disease. A new study looked at more than 1300 men and women divided into three groups: one group comprised patients with amnestic mild cognitive impairment; the second group included patients with Alzheimer's dementia; and the final group included healthy controls. The researchers measured glucose metabolic rates with PET scans. Participants were then given immediate and delayed verbal recall tests.
Women with either no, mild or moderate problems performed better than men on the verbal memory tests. There was no difference in those with advanced Alzheimer's.
Because verbal memory scores are used for diagnosing Alzheimer's, some women may be further along in their disease before they are diagnosed. This suggests the need to have an increased index of suspicion when evaluating women with memory problems.

Part C

In this part of the test, there are two texts about different aspects of healthcare. For **questions 7-22**, choose the answer (**A**, **B**, **C** or **D**) which you think fits best according to the text.

Text 1: Asbestosis

Asbestos is a naturally occurring mineral that has been linked to human lung disease. It has been used in a huge number of products due to its high tensile strength, relative resistance to acid and temperature, and its varying textures and degrees of flexibility. It does not evaporate, dissolve, burn or undergo significant reactions with other chemicals. Because of the widespread use of asbestos, its fibres are **ubiquitous** in the environment. Building insulation materials manufactured since 1975 should no longer contain asbestos; however, products made or stockpiled before this time remain in many homes. Indoor air may become contaminated with fibres released from building materials, especially if they are damaged or crumbling.

One of the three types of asbestos-related diseases is asbestosis, a process of lung tissue scarring caused by asbestos fibres. The symptoms of asbestosis usually include slowly progressing shortness of breath and cough, often 20 to 40 years after exposure. Breathlessness advances throughout the disease, even without further asbestos inhalation. This fact is highlighted in the case of a 67-year-old retired plumber. He was on ramipril to treat his hypertension and developed a persistent dry cough, which his doctor presumed to be an ACE inhibitor induced cough. The ramipril was changed to losartan. The patient had never smoked and did not have a history of asthma or COPD. His cough worsened and he complained of breathlessness on exertion. In view of this history and the fact that he was a non-smoker, he was referred for a chest X-ray and to the local respiratory physician. His doctor was surprised to learn that the patient had asbestosis, diagnosed by a high-resolution CT scan. The patient then began legal proceedings to claim compensation as he had worked in a dockyard 25 years previously, during which time he was exposed to asbestos.

There are two major groups of asbestos fibres, the amphibole and chrysotile fibres. The amphiboles are much more likely to cause cancer of the lining of the lung (mesothelioma) and scarring of the lining of the lung (pleural fibrosis). Either group of fibres can cause disease of the lung, such as asbestosis. The risk of developing asbestos-related lung cancer varies between fibre types. Studies of groups of patients exposed to chrysotile fibres show only a moderate increase in risk. On the other hand, exposure to amphibole fibres or to both types of fibres increases the risk of lung cancer two-fold. Although the Occupational Safety and Health Administration (OSHA) has a standard for workplace exposure to asbestos (0.2 fibres/millilitre of air), there is debate over what constitutes a safe level of exposure. While some believe asbestos-related disease is a 'threshold phenomenon', which requires a certain level of exposure for disease to occur, others believe there is no safe level of asbestos.

Depending on their shape and size, asbestos fibres deposit in different areas of the lung. Fibres less than 3mm easily move into the lung tissue and the lining surrounding the lung. Long fibres, greater than 5mm cannot be completely broken down by scavenger cells (macrophages) and become lodged in the lung tissue, causing inflammation. Substances damaging to the lungs are then released by cells that are responding to the foreign asbestos material. The persistence of these long fibres in the lung tissue and the resulting inflammation seem to initiate the process of cancer formation. As inflammation and damage to tissue around the asbestos fibres continues, the resulting scarring can extend from the small airways to the larger airways and the tiny air sacs (alveoli) at the end of the airways.

There is no cure for asbestosis. Treatments focus on a patient's ability to breathe. Medications like bronchodilators, aspirin and antibiotics are often prescribed and such treatments as oxygen therapy and postural drainage may be recommended. If symptoms are so severe that medications don't work, surgery may be recommended to remove scar tissue. Patients with asbestosis, like others with chronic lung disease, are at a higher risk of serious infections that take advantage of diseased or scarred lung tissue, so prevention and rapid treatment is vital. Flu and pneumococcal vaccinations are a part of routine care for these patients. Patients with progressive disease may be given corticosteroids and cyclophosphamide with limited improvement.

Chrysotile is the only form of asbestos that is currently in production today. Despite their association with lung cancer, chrysotile products are still used in 60 countries, according to the industry-sponsored Asbestos Institute. Although the asbestos industry proclaims the 'safety' of chrysotile fibres, which are now imbedded in less friable and 'dusty' products, little is known about the long term effects of these products because of the long delay in the development of disease. In spite of their potential health risks, the durability and cheapness of these products continue to attract commercial applications. Asbestosis remains a significant clinical problem even after marked reductions in on-the-job exposure to asbestos. Again, **this** is due to the long period of time between exposure and the onset of disease.

Text 1: Questions 7-14

7. The writer suggests that the potential for harm from asbestos is increased by

   - A. a change in the method of manufacture.
   - B. the way it reacts with other substances.
   - C. the fact that it is used so extensively.
   - D. its presence in recently constructed buildings.

8. The word '**ubiquitous**' in paragraph one suggests that asbestos fibres

   - A. can be found everywhere.
   - B. may last for a long time.
   - C. have an unchanging nature.
   - D. are a natural substance.

9. The case study of the 67-year-old man is given to show that

   - A. smoking is unrelated to a diagnosis of asbestosis.
   - B. doctors should be able to diagnose asbestosis earlier.
   - C. the time from exposure to disease may cause delayed diagnosis.
   - D. patients must provide full employment history details to their doctors.

10. In the third paragraph, the writer highlights the disagreement about

    - A. the relative safety of the two types of asbestos fibres.
    - B. the impact of types of fibres on disease development.
    - C. the results of studies into the levels of risk of fibre types.
    - D. the degree of contact with asbestos fibres considered harmful.

11. In the fourth paragraph, the writer points out that longer asbestos fibres

   A) can travel as far as the alveoli.
   B) tend to remain in the pulmonary tissue.
   C) release substances causing inflammation.
   D) mount a defence against the body's macrophages.

12. What is highlighted as an important component of patient management?

   A) the use of corticosteroids
   B) infection control
   C) early intervention
   D) excision of scarred tissue

13. The writer states that products made from chrysotile

   A) have restricted application.
   B) may pose a future health threat.
   C) enjoy approval by the regulatory bodies.
   D) are safer than earlier asbestos-containing products.

14. In the final paragraph, the word 'this' refers to

   A) the interval from asbestos exposure to disease.
   B) the decreased use of asbestos in workplaces.
   C) asbestosis as an ongoing medical issue.
   D) occupational exposure to asbestos.

Text 2: Medication non-compliance

A US doctor gives his views on a new program

An important component of a patient's history and physical examination is the question of 'medication compliance,' the term used by physicians to designate whether, or not, a patient is taking his or her medications. Many a hospital chart bears the notorious comment 'Patient has a history of non-compliance.' Now, under a new experimental program in Philadelphia, USA, patients are being paid to take their medications. The concept makes sense in theory - failure to comply is one of the most common reasons that patients are readmitted to hospital shortly after being discharged.

Compliant patients take their medications because they want to live as long as possible; some simply do so because they're responsible, conscientious individuals by nature. But the hustle and bustle of daily life and employment often get in the way of taking medications, especially those that are timed inconveniently or in frequent doses, even for such well-intentioned patients. For the elderly and the mentally or physically impaired, US insurance companies will often pay for a daily visit by a nurse, to ensure a patient gets at least one set of the most vital pills. But other patients are left to fend for themselves, and it is not uncommon these days for patients to be taking a considerable number of vital pills daily.

Some patients have not been properly educated about the importance of their medications in layman's terms. They have told me, for instance, that they don't have high blood pressure because they were once prescribed a high blood pressure pill – in essence, they view an antihypertensive as an antibiotic that can be used as short-term treatment for a short-term problem. Others have told me that they never had a heart attack because they were taken to the cardiac catheterization lab and 'fixed.' As physicians we are responsible for making sure patients understand their own medical history and their own medications.

Not uncommonly patients will say, 'I googled it the other day, and there was a long list of side effects.' But a simple conversation with the patient at this juncture can easily change their perspective. As with many things in medicine, it's all about risks versus benefits – that's what we as physicians are trained to analyse. And patients can rest assured that we'll monitor them closely for side effects and address any that are unpleasant, either by treating them or by trying a different medication.

But to return to the program in Philadelphia, my firm belief is that if patients don't have strong enough incentives to take their medications so they can live longer, healthier lives, then the long-term benefits of providing a financial incentive are likely to be minimal. At the outset, the rewards may be substantial enough to elicit a response. But one isolated system or patient study is not an accurate depiction of the real-life scenario: patients will have to be taking these medications for decades.

Although a simple financial incentives program has its appeal, its complications abound. What's worse, it seems to be saying to society: as physicians, we tell our patients that not only do we work to care for them, but we'll now pay them to take better care of themselves. And by the way, for all you medication-compliant patients out there, you can have the inherent reward of a longer, healthier life, but we're not going to bother sending you money. This seems like some sort of implied punishment.

But more generally, what advice can be given to doctors with non-compliant patients? Dr John Steiner has written a paper on the matter: 'Be compassionate,' he urges doctors. 'Understand what a complicated balancing act it is for patients.' He's surely right **on that score**. Doctors and patients need to work together to figure out what is reasonable and realistic, prioritizing which measures are most important. For one patient, taking the diabetes pills might be more crucial than trying to quit smoking. For another, treating depression is more critical than treating cholesterol. 'Improving compliance is a team sport,' Dr Steiner adds. 'Input from nurses, care managers, social workers and pharmacists is critical.'

When discussing the complicated nuances of compliance with my students, I give the example of my grandmother. A thrifty, no-nonsense woman, she routinely sliced all the cholesterol and heart disease pills her doctor prescribed in half, taking only half the dose. If I questioned this, she'd wave me off with, 'What do those doctors know, anyway?' Sadly, she died suddenly, aged 87, most likely of a massive heart attack. Had she taken her medicines at the appropriate doses, she might have survived it. But then maybe she'd have died a more painful death from some other ailment. Her biggest fear had always been ending up dependent in a nursing home, and by luck or design, she was able to avoid that. Perhaps there was some wisdom in her 'non-compliance.'

Text 2: Questions 15-22

15. In the first paragraph, what is the writer's attitude towards the new programme?

- A) He doubts that it is correctly named.
- B) He appreciates the reasons behind it.
- C) He is sceptical about whether it can work.
- D) He is more enthusiastic than some other doctors.

16. In the second paragraph, the writer suggests that one category of non-compliance is

- A) elderly patients who are given occasional assistance.
- B) patients who are over-prescribed with a certain drug.
- C) busy working people who mean to be compliant.
- D) people who are by nature wary of taking pills.

17. What problem with some patients is described in the third paragraph?

- A) They forget which prescribed medication is for which of their conditions.
- B) They fail to recognise that some medical conditions require ongoing treatment.
- C) They don't understand their treatment even when it's explained in simple terms.
- D) They believe that taking some prescribed pills means they don't need to take others.

18. What does the writer say about side effects to medication?

- A) Doctors need to have better plans in place if they develop.
- B) There is too much misleading information about them online.
- C) Fear of them can waste a lot of unnecessary consultation time.
- D) Patients need to be informed about the likelihood of them occurring.

19. In the fifth paragraph, what is the writer's reservation about the Philadelphia program?

   A. the long-term feasibility of the central idea

   B. the size of the financial incentives offered

   C. the types of medication that were targeted

   D. the particular sample chosen to participate

20. What objection to the program does the writer make in the sixth paragraph?

   A. It will be counter-productive.

   B. It will place heavy demands on doctors.

   C. It sends the wrong message to patients.

   D. It is a simplistic idea that falls down on its details.

21. The expression '**on that score**' in the seventh paragraph refers to

   A. a complex solution to patients' problems.

   B. a co-operative attitude amongst medical staff.

   C. a realistic assessment of why something happens.

   D. a recommended response to the concerns of patients.

22. The writer suggests that his grandmother

   A. may ultimately have benefited from her non-compliance.

   B. would have appreciated closer medical supervision.

   C. might have underestimated how ill she was.

   D. should have followed her doctor's advice.

END OF READING TEST
THIS BOOKLET WILL BE COLLECTED

WRITING SUB-TEST – TEST BOOKLET

CANDIDATE NUMBER:
LAST NAME:
FIRST NAME:
MIDDLE NAMES:
PROFESSION:
VENUE:
TEST DATE:

Candidate details and photo will be printed here.

Passport Photo

CANDIDATE DECLARATION

By signing this, you agree not to disclose or use in any way (other than to take the test) or assist any other person to disclose or use any OET test or sub-test content. If you cheat or assist in any cheating, use any unfair practice, break any of the rules or regulations, or ignore any advice or information, you may be disqualified and your results may not be issued at the sole discretion of CBLA. CBLA also reserves its right to take further disciplinary action against you and to pursue any other remedies permitted by law. If a candidate is suspected of and investigated for malpractice, their personal details and details of the investigation may be passed to a third party where required.

CANDIDATE SIGNATURE: _____

INSTRUCTIONS TO CANDIDATES

You must write your answer for the Writing sub-test in the **Writing Answer Booklet.**

You must **NOT** remove OET material from the test room.

www.occupationalenglishtest.org
© Cambridge Boxhill Language Assessment – ABN 51 988 559 414

[CANDIDATE NO.] WRITING SUB-TEST TEST BOOKLET 01/04

OCCUPATIONAL ENGLISH TEST

WRITING SUB-TEST: MEDICINE

TIME ALLOWED: READING TIME: 5 MINUTES
WRITING TIME: 40 MINUTES

Read the case notes below and complete the writing task which follows.

Notes:

Mr Brett Collister is a male patient in your general practice.

PATIENT DETAILS:

Name:	Mr Brett Collister (DOB: 21 December 1973)
Height:	177cm
Occupation:	Factory foreman
Social background:	Married, 3 children (18, 16, 13 yrs)
Hobbies:	Watching football, playing darts, fishing
Medical history:	No known allergies
	Infectious mononucleosis – February 2006

Treatment record

22/04/18
Productive cough & sore throat for 1 week, green phlegm
Pt tired, temp (38°C)

Treatment: Rest, plenty of fluids, salt water gargles

26/06/18
Sore throat – suddenly worse after 3 weeks of intermittent pain & fever; Pt feels 'run-down'
Tonsils inflamed; temp 38.5°C

Treatment: Prescribed amoxicillin

17/09/18
Sore L shoulder – triggered during game of darts 2 weeks previous – ?rotator cuff tear
Busy at work – feels tired & stressed

Treatment: Prescribed ibuprofen
R.I.C.E. (rest, ice, compression, elevation)
Refer to physio for exercise program & treatment for shoulder

26/11/18
Sore R knee – pain intermittent, worse going up stairs. No identified trigger
?osteoarthritis
Shoulder has improved
BP 107/60, HR 78 (reg), Wt 94kg (BMI 30 – overweight)

Treatment: Prescribed ibuprofen
Advised to ↓ weight, ↑ exercise (cycling, swimming)
Refer to physio (as previously) – review in 3 months

04/02/19	Pt feels tired, 'run-down'; sore eyes, dizzy sometimes (for last 3-4 weeks) – ?orthostatic hypotension
	Overweight, unfit – no adjustment to lifestyle, diet, exercise
	Reports busy at work
	BP 108/61, HR 80 (reg), lungs clear, Wt 93kg (BMI 29.7 – overweight)
	Treatment: Order blood tests to review cholesterol, blood sugars, etc.
24/02/19	Still tired, sore eyes, vision↓
	BP 105/60, HR 78 (reg), lungs clear, Wt 89kg (BMI 28.4 – overweight)
	Review of tests organised 04/02/18:
	• random glucose 13.5mmol/L (high)
	• fasting glucose 7.4mmol/L (high)
	• HbA1c 8.5% (high)
	• HDL/LDL ↑ (cholesterol 6.4mmol/L, LDL 4.2mmol/L, HDL 2.1mmol/L, Trig 3.3mmol/L)
	Preliminary diagnosis: Results indicate DM (diabetes mellitus) Type 2
	Treatment: Refer to endocrinologist for assessment and management plan

Writing Task:

Using the information in the case notes, write a letter of referral to Dr Grantley Cross, an endocrinologist, requesting assessment and a management plan. Address your letter to Dr Grantley Cross, Consultant Endocrinologist, City Hospital, Suite 32, 55 Main Road, Newtown.

In your answer:
- **Expand the relevant notes into complete sentences**
- **Do not use note form**
- **Use letter format**

The body of the letter should be approximately 180–200 words.

WRITING SUB-TEST – ANSWER BOOKLET

CANDIDATE NUMBER:

LAST NAME:

FIRST NAME:

MIDDLE NAMES:

PROFESSION: Candidate details and photo will be printed here.

VENUE:

TEST DATE:

Passport Photo

CANDIDATE DECLARATION

By signing this, you agree not to disclose or use in any way (other than to take the test) or assist any other person to disclose or use any OET test or sub-test content. If you cheat or assist in any cheating, use any unfair practice, break any of the rules or regulations, or ignore any advice or information, you may be disqualified and your results may not be issued at the sole discretion of CBLA. CBLA also reserves its right to take further disciplinary action against you and to pursue any other remedies permitted by law. If a candidate is suspected of and investigated for malpractice, their personal details and details of the investigation may be passed to a third party where required.

CANDIDATE SIGNATURE: _____

TIME ALLOWED
READING TIME: 5 MINUTES
WRITING TIME: 40 MINUTES

INSTRUCTIONS TO CANDIDATES

1. **Reading time: 5 minutes**
   During this time you may study the writing task and notes. You **MUST NOT** write, highlight, underline or make any notes.

2. **Writing time: 40 minutes**

3. Use the back page for notes and rough draft only. Notes and rough draft will **NOT** be marked.

   Please write your answer clearly on page 1 and page 2.

   Cross out anything you **DO NOT** want the examiner to consider.

4. You must write your answer for the Writing sub-test in this **Answer Booklet** using **pen or pencil**.

5. You must **NOT** remove OET material from the test room.

www.occupationalenglishtest.org
© Cambridge Boxhill Language Assessment – ABN 51 988 559 414

[CANDIDATE NO.] WRITING SUB-TEST ANSWER BOOKLET 01/04

 50 PRACTICE TEST 1

Please record your answer on this page.
(Only answers on Page 1 and Page 2 will be marked.)

OET Writing sub-test – Answer booklet 1

Please record your answer on this page.

(Only answers on Page 1 and Page 2 will be marked.)

OET Writing sub-test – Answer booklet 2

[CANDIDATE NO.] WRITING SUB-TEST - ANSWER BOOKLET 03/04

Space for notes and rough draft. Only your answers on Page 1 and Page 2 will be marked.

SPEAKING SUB-TEST

CANDIDATE NUMBER:
LAST NAME:
FIRST NAME:
MIDDLE NAMES:
PROFESSION:
VENUE:
TEST DATE:

Your details and photo will be printed here.

Passport Photo

CANDIDATE DECLARATION
By signing this, you agree not to disclose or use in any way (other than to take the test) or assist any other person to disclose or use any OET test or sub-test content. If you cheat or assist in any cheating, use any unfair practice, break any of the rules or regulations, or ignore any advice or information, you may be disqualified and your results may not be issued at the sole discretion of CBLA. CBLA also reserves its right to take further disciplinary action against you and to pursue any other remedies permitted by law. If a candidate is suspected of and investigated for malpractice, their personal details and details of the investigation may be passed to a third party where required.

CANDIDATE SIGNATURE: _____

INSTRUCTION TO CANDIDATES
Please confirm with the Interlocutor that your roleplay card number and colour match the Interlocutor card before you begin.

Interlocutor to complete only

ID No: _____ Passport: ☐   National ID: ☐   Alternative ID approved: ☐

Speaking sub-test:
ID document sighted? ☐   Photo match? ☐   Signature match? ☐   Did not attend? ☐

Interlocutor name: _____
Interlocutor signature: _____

www.occupationalenglishtest.org
© Cambridge Boxhill Language Assessment – ABN 51 988 559 414
[CANDIDATE NO.] SPEAKING SUB-TEST 01/04

OET Sample role-play

ROLEPLAYER CARD NO. 1 — MEDICINE

SETTING: Suburban Clinic

PATIENT: You have had a fright: you had a bad bout of flu recently and you feel increasingly short of breath. You also complain of a dry throat. This morning you thought you were going to die, as you couldn't catch your breath. You are worried that it is asthma.

TASK:
- When asked about asthma, state that you want to know what causes it, and how it can be treated.
- Express concern about the proposal to use Ventolin, as people have told you about its misuse.
- Express anxiety about your condition. You've heard stories of people dying from asthma attacks.

© Cambridge Boxhill Language Assessment — Sample role-play

OET Sample role-play

CANDIDATE CARD NO. 1 — MEDICINE

SETTING: Suburban Clinic

DOCTOR: The patient came to you with flu recently and has now presented with acute shortness of breath. You diagnose asthma.

TASK:
- Find out what the patient knows about asthma.
- Explain the causes of asthma (e.g., environmental factors, inherited predisposition, etc.).
- Discuss the treatment (Ventolin – salbutamol).
- Reassure the patient about the safety of Ventolin.
- Deal with the patient's anxiety about the problem, emphasising that it can be controlled and discuss the prognosis for asthma patients.

© Cambridge Boxhill Language Assessment — Sample role-play

OET Sample role-play

ROLEPLAYER CARD NO. 2   **MEDICINE**

SETTING: Suburban Clinic

PARENT: Your six-year-old daughter has been home from school because she has developed a rash with mild fever over the past three days. Large spots are appearing on her body and the child is feeling lethargic with loss of appetite. She is also scratching the spots, which are itchy.

Principally, the course of disease is mild

TASK:
- When asked, you want to know if chickenpox is dangerous or if it is contagious.
- You have a ten-month-old son: will he catch it? Is it dangerous for a young child?
- If it is not mentioned, find out when the child can return to school.
- When asked, you want to know how you can stop the child scratching the spots.

The virus is transmitted by airborne droplets, it means through face-to-face contact with a sick person, as well as through contaminated surfaces and objects.
via droplets and saliva [saliva]

© Cambridge Boxhill Language Assessment   Sample role-play

OET Sample role-play

CANDIDATE CARD NO. 2   **MEDICINE**

SETTING: Suburban Clinic

DOCTOR: A six-year-old girl has been brought in by her parent with a three-day history of rash and mild fever. Physical examination reveals obvious chickenpox (varicella zoster). Apart from the rash and mild fever, there are no signs of complications.

course - mebiep
children's age - week during

TASK:
- Explain to the parent that the child has chickenpox. Find out what information the parent wants to know.
- Discuss management as the condition is contagious and can last two to three weeks. The child must be kept home from school until the spots have formed scabs (usually about a week).
- Outline the ways to reduce itching: ensure loose cotton clothing to allow the skin to breathe, calamine lotion, and antihistamines, like Benadryl, can be appropriate.
- Advise the parent that the child should return for review if any new or unusual symptoms arise.

© Cambridge Boxhill Language Assessment   Sample role-play

 56   PRACTICE TEST 1

Listening sub-test
ANSWER KEY – Parts A, B & C

LISTENING SUB-TEST – ANSWER KEY

PART A: QUESTIONS 1-12

1. (computer) programmer
2. asthma (attacks)
3. penicillin
4. vegetarian
5. fertility
6. breech
7. forceps / forcipes
8. breastfeeding
9. epilepsy
10. Down syndrome / DS / DNS / Down's (syndrome)
11. CVS / chronic vill(o)us sampling
12. sibling(s) / brothers and/or sisters

PART A: QUESTIONS 13-24

13. medial meniscus OR medial
14. (very tender/tender/painful) bumps
15. squat (properly) / bend (his) knee
16. (used) ice pack(s)
17. tendonitis
18. (hospital) physio(therapist) / physio(therapist) (in the hospital)
19. hamstring(s)
20. (constant) anxiety
21. fibromyalgia
22. (a pain/pain) diary
23. (his) shoulders and elbows / (his) elbows and shoulders
24. rheumatologist

PART B: QUESTIONS 25-30

25. A correcting patient's misconception about obesity
26. B getting approval for a repair to a machine.
27. A locate the CPR board quickly enough.
28. B there is sensory loss in her legs.
29. C She values the greater understanding it gives her of her work.
30. A the age of the subjects.

PART C: QUESTIONS 31-36

31. A she was considering retirement from her sport.
32. C some key muscles weren't strong enough.
33. B soon discovered what was causing the problem.
34. C The treatment was succeeding without it.
35. B focussed on applying the correct techniques.
36. B to reduce the stress placed on her take-off leg

PART C: QUESTIONS 37-42

37. A where it was originally published
38. A gain insights into their mental health problems.
39. C a tendency to jump to conclusions
40. A They provide an insight not gained from numbers alone.
41. C He is doubtful of their value when used independently.
42. B his commitment to making them more widely accepted.

END OF KEY

Listening sub-test
Audio Script – Practice test 1

OCCUPATIONAL ENGLISH TEST. PRACTICE TEST 1. LISTENING TEST.

This test has three parts. In each part you'll hear a number of different extracts. At the start of each extract, you'll hear this sound: ---***---.

You'll have time to read the questions before you hear each extract and you'll hear each extract ONCE only. Complete your answers as you listen.

At the end of the test, you'll have two minutes to check your answers.

Part A. In this part of the test, you'll hear two different extracts. In each extract, a health professional is talking to a patient. For questions 1 to 24, complete the notes with information you hear. Now, look at the notes for extract one.

PAUSE: 5 SECONDS
Extract one. Questions 1 to 12.

You hear an obstetrician talking to a patient called Melissa Gordon. For questions 1 to 12, complete the notes with a word or short phrase. You now have thirty seconds to look at the notes.

PAUSE: 30 SECONDS

---***---

M: So, this first meeting, Mrs Gordon, is mainly a chance for you and I to get to know each other. I'll ask you about your medical history and this is also an opportunity for you to ask me any questions that you've got at this point.

F: Sure.

M: So, some background. What kind of work do you do?

F: I have a job at an engineering company. I'm a computer programmer. I currently do four days a week, but I hope to reduce that to three after my maternity leave.

M: Ahh, excellent. So tell me about your medical health? Do you have any conditions I should know about?

F: Well err, I have asthma attacks but they don't happen often. I lost about ten kilos and that's certainly helped. I have an inhaler but I hardly ever use it. Oh, I should also let you know that I come out in terrible hives if I take penicillin, but not other things - I'm fine if I eat nuts, for example. I have a fairly healthy lifestyle. I'm a vegetarian and I've never smoked.

M: Good.

F: I'm afraid I don't go to the gym or anything, but I walk to work and err… generally keep active.

M: Ahh that's good. So is this your first pregnancy?

F: No, I have a daughter called Ella – she's three now.

M: Ahh…and did everything go smoothly that time?

F: There were no major problems during the pregnancy itself. But it took me quite a time to fall pregnant - the first time. After having various tests, I was given some fertility drugs. Ohh what were they called? It's on the tip of my tongue. Ahm, never mind. It'll come back to me. This time, though, I didn't need any help.

M: It's no problem. What about labour last time around?

F: That was a nightmare…though everything - thank goodness - worked out in the end. It was a breech birth. It looked as if I might have to have a caesarean, and I really didn't want that. I was pleased I managed without an epidural too. They had to use forceps to get Ella out but I didn't need any stitches, so that was OK. Unfortunately, though, I had some difficulties after the birth too. I was desperate to start breastfeeding, but that didn't work out - at least not until I was given some guidance by the midwife.

M: OK. So can I ask you about the baby's father?

F: Sure. That's my husband, Paul. There's something in his family history I should tell you about, I think. His grandfather and father both had epilepsy - though he hasn't developed it himself. I'm not sure if that means his children have a greater chance of having it or not. Oh, also he has a child from his first marriage and she has Down's syndrome. So he gets a bit anxious when I'm pregnant.

M: Oh well, that's understandable, of course. We can discuss various testing options if you like. You might want to consider amniocentesis, for instance.

F: But that carries a risk of miscarriage, doesn't it? I don't want to go for that. I've heard about another test called err…CVS. Is that something to consider?

M: Well, it's certainly an option. However, that procedure in fact also carries a small increase in the risk of miscarriage. And you'd need to come to a decision fairly soon, because it's normally carried out between weeks…ten and twelve of the pregnancy.

F: Well, I can tell you straightaway that if there's more risk then I wouldn't consider it. I know my husband will feel the same.

M: Well that's fair enough. So, is there anything else you'd like to ask me about today?

F: Nothing urgent. But it'd be good to know more about how to get siblings ready for a new addition to the family. I want to make sure Ella doesn't feel threatened or replaced or anything.

M: Well, there's a leaflet that many parents find helpful. Here we are - have a look through that.

F: Ahh, thanks – that's great. I'm sure I'll have lots more questions at our next meeting.

PAUSE: 10 SECONDS
Extract two. Questions 13 to 24.

You hear a GP talking to a new patient called Mike Royce. For questions 13 to 24, complete the notes with a word or short phrase. You now have thirty seconds to look at the notes.

PAUSE: 30 SECONDS
---***---

F   Hello. Come on in. You must be Mr Royce. I understand that you've just signed up with the practice.

M   Yeah that's right, Mike Royce. I've joined this practice because my previous GP retired and he suggested I come here.

F   Right, and I understand you've got an ongoing medical condition you're worried about. Perhaps you'd like to start by telling me about that. How did it start?

M	Well, I suppose it started out as a really strong pain in my left knee, in, um, I think it's called the… the medial meniscus. Is that right? It came on whenever I tried to bend the knee more than normal. Then I tripped while climbing some stairs at work and that seemed to make things worse. I started to get these very tender bumps all over the back of the knee. They were very painful, even just lightly touching them. The doctor called them trigger points.
F	*Yeah, that's right. They're called that because pain frequently radiates out from them when touched. And how did that affect you day-to-day?*
M	Well, I went back to work after a week or so, but I was still having knee problems. I couldn't really squat properly or climb ladders – that's important in my job. I'm a painter, you know, and I'm always having to get into awkward positions. Anyway, I kept going back to my old GP explaining that I still had severe pain whenever I tried to bend my knee. He gave me all these exercises to do, and I tried doing them, I really did. I made sure I did gentle stretches before I did anything more energetic, everything really. I tried resting like he told me, I used ice packs when, when it got sore, but nothing really worked.
F	*Right, I see…*
M	But then the doctor decided I might be suffering from tendonitis, so he sent me for some rehab work in the hospital. That actually did seem to work, at least at first.
F	*But I'm guessing not for long.*
M	Right. The problem came back. I kept telling the doctor that my knee still wasn't healed, but it was actually my physiotherapist in the hospital rather than my old GP who noticed that something was wrong with my muscles. He wouldn't say what it was, but I knew something was up. He was doing myofascial release on my hamstrings and I was in agony.
F	*Right, so did…did you go back to your GP?*
M	I did. But he didn't know what I should do about it. So I left feeling completely fed up. That's one of the reasons I decided to come here. I just feel like nobody's taking this seriously. I think it's affecting my life in lots of other ways too. The worry's giving me insomnia for one thing. I don't think I have actual depression, but I certainly suffer from constant anxiety about when it's going to flare up.
F	*Is there anything that you're particularly worried you might have?*
M	Well, I've researched this pain I'm getting. Erm, to be honest, I'm convinced I've got fibromyalgia, not just some simple muscle problem, because I fit most of the symptoms, and I've had pain absolutely everywhere. Look. I've even kept a… a pain diary so that I could track what I did that set it off, you know, the weather, if I was working or not, where it was affecting me, what it felt like. I've figured out from this that it's usually in the same places that I mentioned earlier, plus some newish places too… my shoulders and elbows – and I know that my knee's actually one of the more tender points for it. What do you think?
F	*Look, I must say from what you've told me so far that I'm concerned enough to look into that possibility. So, as a next step, we need to get you seen by a rheumatologist. This is a notoriously difficult condition to diagnose, as I'm sure you're aware, because so many of the symptoms overlap with other conditions too.*
M	I won't be happy to be proved right but I'll certainly be glad to get some answers at long last.

PAUSE: 10 SECONDS
That is the end of Part A. Now, look at Part B.

PAUSE: 5 SECONDS

Part B.

In this part of the test, you'll hear six different extracts. In each extract, you'll hear people talking in a different healthcare setting.

For questions 25 to 30, choose the answer A, B or C which fits best according to what you hear. You'll have time to read each question before you listen. Complete your answers as you listen.

Now look at Question 25. You hear a dietitian talking to a patient. Now read the question.

PAUSE: 15 SECONDS

---***---

F: So what seems to be the problem?

M: I feel such a failure. I'm sure people think that if I just tried harder, I could lose weight. Maybe I need more willpower.

F: Well, firstly, well done for seeking medical help. Actually, being overweight or obese is a medical problem, because being overweight changes how your body works.

M: Oh, thanks, but I do feel that it's my fault for being this way.

F: Well, I hear what you say, but please understand that these days, we consider that obesity is a disease, like high blood pressure or asthma. You see, the body's signals to the brain stop working correctly when you're overweight. And, with time, you feel less full, even if you eat the same amount. And when you cut calories, your body tries to use less energy to keep your weight the same.

PAUSE: 5 SECONDS

Question 26. You hear members of a hospital committee discussing problems in the X-ray department. Now read the question.

PAUSE: 15 SECONDS

---***---

F: So next on the agenda is the problems in the X-ray department. Nick, would you like to fill us in here?

M: Well, as you all know, this is a very busy department. Err, so we have four X-ray machines in all, including one in the Fracture and Orthopaedic clinic area, but recently one of the other X-ray machines developed a fault and so we had to apply for authorisation for the purchase of a new tube for it. There's been some kind of hold up with the paperwork, and while we've been waiting, patients are being brought into the Fracture and Orthopaedic area for X-rays there instead, and of course that's causing further congestion.

PAUSE: 5 SECONDS

Question 27. You hear a senior nurse giving feedback to a trainee after a training exercise. Now read the question.

PAUSE: 15 SECONDS

---***---

F	OK, that went quite well, didn't it? But it took you a while to work out where the CPR board was kept. So what does that tell you about this scenario?
M	We need to check where things are before doing anything else.
F	Exactly. And of course it takes a second or two to put the head of the bed down, because you've got to have that part of the bed flat before you slip the board in. I wish there was a quicker way.
M	So do I put the CPR board under, or would I normally hand it over to somebody else?
F	It makes no difference as long as it's done.

PAUSE: 5 SECONDS

Question 28. You hear a trainee nurse asking his senior colleague about the use of anti-embolism socks for a patient. Now read the question.

PAUSE: 15 SECONDS

---***---

M:	I noticed that Mrs Jones isn't wearing the usual anti-embolism socks, but I didn't want to ask her why not because she was asleep. Is it because her legs are swollen?
F:	Well, sometimes we don't recommend the socks if there's severe swelling with oedema, but that's not the case here. Mrs Jones was actually given them initially on admission last night, but she told us this morning that her lower legs were feeling numb – she described it as having no feeling. Until we've checked out the reason for that, for example it could be an underlying condition which could damage her arterial circulation, we're reducing the risk of thrombosis by pharmacological means.
M:	Oh, I see.

PAUSE: 5 SECONDS

Question 29. You hear a vet talking about her involvement in the management of the practice where she works. Now read the question.

PAUSE: 15 SECONDS

---***---

F:	At first, when I took over the financial running of the practice, I felt rather thrown in at the deep end. I really needed to know my stuff and be super organised, especially with the number of new drugs and treatments available now, all of which have to be very carefully costed. It keeps me super-busy, but monitoring stocks and so on helps give me confidence and allows me to see how everything fits into the overall picture of working as a vet. My manager's more than happy to leave me to run this side of things – he's in overall charge, of course, but I can always go to him if there's a problem. I keep him closely informed of what's happening. He's always pleased if I manage to make savings anywhere.

PAUSE: 5 SECONDS

Question 30. You hear a physiotherapist giving a presentation about a study she's been involved in. Now read the question.

PAUSE: 15 SECONDS
---***---

F: I'm a physiotherapist, and I'm presenting our poster about constraint induced movement therapy for children suffering from partial paralysis following brain surgery.

We did a case series of four children, who'd all undergone hemispherectomies. They were admitted to inpatient therapy within two weeks post-op and began therapy two to three weeks post-op. The therapy continued after they were discharged. Our findings were that three of the kids regained excellent function and mobility with ambulation and upper extremity function. One didn't do so well, unfortunately, but he gave up the therapy early on. This type of movement therapy has been used a lot in adult populations following stroke. The findings here promote moving forward with further research on the paediatric or adolescent population, following either hemispherectomy or other surgeries, to help us decide how appropriate this therapy would be for them.

PAUSE: 10 SECONDS
That is the end of Part B. Now, look at Part C.

PAUSE: 5 SECONDS
Part C. In this part of the test, you'll hear two different extracts. In each extract, you'll hear health professionals talking about aspects of their work.

For questions 31 to 42, choose the answer A, B or C which fits best according to what you hear. Complete your answers as you listen.

Now look at extract one.

Extract one. Questions 31 to 36. You hear a sports physiotherapist called Chris Maloney giving a presentation in which he describes treating a high jumper with a knee injury.

You now have 90 seconds to read questions 31 to 36.

PAUSE: 90 SECONDS
---***---

M: Hello. I'm Chris Maloney, a physiotherapist specialising in sports injuries, and I'd like to present a case study to give you an idea of the sort of work I do.

It features a very successful high jumper in her mid-twenties, who was referred to me with severe pain in her right knee – and that's the leg she takes off from when she jumps. What's more, when she'd stepped up her training in preparation for a big competition, the pain worsened, and she'd been forced to pull out of the event. After that, she'd taken several months off training to rest and get treatment from various therapists. To her dismay, however, not only did the pain continue, it actually got worse, meaning she was unable to do any strength training, let alone jump-specific work. By the time I saw her, she was on the verge of giving up, having lost virtually all belief in her ability.

My initial assessment quickly confirmed patellar tendinitis in the affected knee, accompanied by some swelling and significant tenderness over the lower part of the kneecap – this wasn't difficult to diagnose. I also noted that she was slightly overweight for her height and had rather flat feet, but that's not so unusual in high jumpers. Further assessment revealed that the gluteal muscles connecting the hips and thighs were considerably less sturdy than you'd expect in an athlete of this calibre, and both the lateral retinaculum connecting the patella to the femur and the ilio-tibial band – the ligament running down the outside of the thigh – were tight and tender.

As a first stage, I was keen to show I could help by relieving some of the pain. So, I worked at loosening her lateral retinaculum to see how much of the tendon pain was due to inflammation and how much came from restriction of normal patellar movement. This manipulation and massage instantly cleared the pain she'd felt while doing a single-leg dip exercise – where you stand on one leg and bend the knee. This indicated that her tendon pain was most likely due to patello-femoral joint dysfunction – caused by muscle imbalance and poor biomechanics – and not by an active inflammatory process or partial tear in her patellar tendon, so an MRI scan wasn't needed. The treatment continued along similar lines for some weeks, with loosening of the lateral retinaculum and deep-tissue massage of the ilio-tibial band and other muscles.

One option at this point was something called 'taping'. This is a way of reducing pain so that athletes can continue with strength exercises. But it seemed clear from early on that we shouldn't put taping on this patient's patella and tendon until she started jumping again. She was getting pain relief and progress simply from the manual techniques, and taping might've led to problems later on. Athletes often become dependent on tape and other accessories. In other words, instead of aiming for one-hundred percent muscle strength and joint position control, they settle for eighty percent plus artificial support.

The patient also had a specially designed programme of gym activities. Although she needed to restore power to those muscles affected by inflammation and tenderness, the priority was to get her posture and alignment right. She started by doing double-leg squats with her back to a wall in front of a mirror so that she could see whether her feet were arched and if her knees were over her feet. She also did squats whilst squeezing a ball between her knees. There was light leg press work, followed by single-leg stance work – first static, then on wobble-boards, and with elastic resistance. She progressed to moving on and off steps, sometimes holding weights, all the time paying close attention to positioning and muscle and joint alignment.

The next stage was to liaise with the patient's coach. She began running – jogging for stamina and then sprint sessions. Work on power was stepped up gradually and included some weightlifting. After some analysis, we also decided to modify her…her run-up to the high-jump bar. By beginning from a wider position and running in with much less of a curve, there was much less of an impact on the ankle, knees and hip, especially in her right jumping leg. Interestingly, the patient reported that remodelling the run-up felt fresh and motivating and helped to reinforce the sense she had of being a reborn athlete. Once the rehabilitation process was complete, she was able to compete without pain and free of any reliance on taping or knee-strapping.

So, before I go on to ….. [fade]

PAUSE: 10 SECONDS
Now look at extract two.

Extract two. Questions 37 to 42. You hear a clinical psychiatrist called Dr Anthony Gibbens giving a presentation about the value of individual patients' experiences and 'stories' in medicine.

You now have 90 seconds to read questions 37 to 42.

PAUSE: 90 SECONDS
---***---

M: Hello. My name's Anthony Gibbens. I'm a clinical psychiatrist and published author. I'd like to talk about something that's relevant to all medical professionals: the use of narratives in medicine.

Let me begin with a case study, sent to me by a colleague who shares my interest in the subject. The study featured a thirty-year-old man who was hospitalised for severe panic attacks. He was treated with 'narcoanalysis' but, feeling no relief, turned to alcohol and endured years of depression and social isolation. Four decades later, he was back in the psychiatric system, but for the first time he was prescribed the antidepressant, Zoloft. Six weeks later, he was discharged because the panic attacks and depression had disappeared. He lived a full life until his death nineteen years later. If the narrative was striking, it was even more so for its inclusion in a medical journal.

Repeatedly, I've been surprised by the impact that even lightly sketched case histories can have on readers. In my first book, I wrote about personality and how it might change on medication. My second was concerned with theories of intimacy. Readers, however, often used the books for a different purpose: identifying depression. Regularly I received and still receive phone calls, people saying 'My husband's just like X', one figure from a clinical example. Other readers wrote to say that they'd recognised themselves. Seeing that they weren't alone gave them hope. Encouragement is another benefit of case description, familiar to us in an age when everyone's writing their biography.

But this isn't to say that stories are a panacea to issues inherent in treating patients, and there can be disadvantages. Consider my experience prescribing Prozac. When certain patients reported feeling 'better than well' after receiving it, I presented these examples, first in essays for psychiatrists and then in my book, where I surrounded the narrative material with accounts of research. In time, my loosely supported descriptions led others to do controlled trials that confirmed the phenomenon. But doctors hadn't waited for those controlled trials. In advance, the better-than-well hypothesis had served as a tentative fact. Treating depression, colleagues looked out for personality change, even aimed for it, even though this wasn't my intended outcome.

This brings me to my next point. Often the knowledge that informs clinical decisions emerges when you stand back from it, like an impressionist painting. What initially seems like randomly scattered information begins to come together, and what you see is the bigger picture. That's where the true worth of anecdote lies. Beyond its role as illustration, hypothesis builder, and low-level guidance for practice, storytelling can act as a modest counterbalance to a narrow focus on data. If we rely solely on 'evidence', we risk moving toward a monoculture whereby patients and their afflictions become reduced to inanimate objects – a result I'd consider unfortunate, since there are many ways to influence people for the better. It's been my hope that, while we wait for conclusive science, stories will preserve diversity in our theories of mind.

My recent reading of outcome trials of antidepressants has strengthened my suspicion that the line between research and storytelling can be fuzzy. In medicine, randomised trials are rarely large enough to provide guidance on their own. Statisticians amalgamate many studies through a technique called meta-analysis. The first step of the process, deciding which data to include, colours the findings. Effectively, the numbers are narrative. Put simply, evidence-based medicine is judgment-based medicine in which randomised trials are carefully assessed and given their due. I don't think we need to be embarrassed about this. Our substantial formal findings require integration. The danger is in pretending otherwise.

I've long felt isolated in embracing the use of narratives in medicine, which is why I warm to the likelihood of narratives being used to inform future medical judgements. It would be unfortunate if medicine moved fully to squeeze the art out of its science by marginalising the narrative. Stories aren't just better at capturing the 'bigger picture' but the smaller picture too. I'm thinking of the article about the depressed man given the drug Zoloft. The degree of transformation in the patient was just as impressive as the length of observation. No formal research can offer a forty-year lead-in or a nineteen-year follow-up. Few studies report on both symptoms and social progress. Research reduces information about many people; narratives retain the texture of life in all its forms. We need storytelling, which is why I'll keep harping on about it until the message gets through.

PAUSE: 10 SECONDS
That is the end of Part C.

You now have two minutes to check your answers.

PAUSE: 120 SECONDS
That is the end of the Listening test.

Reading sub-test
Answer Key – Part A

READING SUB-TEST – ANSWER KEY

PART A: QUESTIONS 1-20

1	A
2	B
3	A
4	D
5	B
6	C
7	B
8	fine bore
9	water-based lubricant
10	tape
11	(a) syringe
12	15-30 minutes/mins OR fifteen-thirty minutes/mins
13	(turn) on(to) left side
14	(to) x-ray (department) OR (to) radiology
15	(a) feeding pump
16	stretch
17	gastroesophageal reflux
18	6/six Fr/French
19	breathlessness
20	(expressed) breast milk

Reading sub-test
Answer Key – Parts B & C

READING SUB-TEST – ANSWER KEY

PART B: QUESTIONS 1-6

1	A	this should be reported.
2	C	communicate their intentions to others.
3	B	best practice procedures
4	A	if non-disclosure could adversely affect those involved
5	A	act as a reminder of their obligations.
6	C	mild dementia in women can remain undiagnosed.

PART C: QUESTIONS 7-14

7	C	the fact that it is used so extensively.
8	A	can be found everywhere.
9	C	the time from exposure to disease may cause delayed diagnosis.
10	D	the degree of contact with asbestos fibres considered harmful.
11	B	tend to remain in the pulmonary tissue.
12	B	infection control
13	B	may pose a future health threat.
14	C	asbestosis as an ongoing medical issue.

PART C: QUESTIONS 15-22

15	B	He appreciates the reasons behind it.
16	C	busy working people who mean to be compliant.
17	B	They fail to recognise that some medical conditions require ongoing treatment.
18	D	Patients need to be informed about the likelihood of them occurring.
19	A	the long-term feasibility of the central idea
20	C	It sends the wrong message to patients.
21	D	a recommended response to the concerns of patients.
22	A	may ultimately have benefited from her non-compliance.

OCCUPATIONAL ENGLISH TEST

WRITING SUB-TEST: MEDICINE

SAMPLE RESPONSE: LETTER OF REFERRAL

Dr Grantley Cross
Consultant Endocrinologist
City Hospital
Suite 32, 55 Main Road
Newtown

24 February 2019

Dear Dr Cross,

Re: Brett Collister
DOB: 21 December 1973

Thank you for seeing Mr Brett Collister, a 44-year-old factory foreman, who presented today complaining of sore eyes and worsening vision. I am concerned that he has been experiencing symptoms consistent with Type 2 diabetes.

Mr Collister was treated twice last year for infections. On 4 February 2019, he presented with low blood pressure (108/61), fatigue, intermittent dizziness (possibly orthostatic hypotension) and sore eyes. As a result, I organised blood tests. The results showed elevated readings in random glucose (13.5mmol/L), fasting glucose (7.4mmol/L) and HbA1c levels (8.5%), which are consistent with Type 2 diabetes.

Mr Collister is overweight (BMI 28.4) and his hobbies are mainly sedentary. He has been seeing a physiotherapist for an exercise program and management of his shoulder and knee, which were causing some pain last year. His job is demanding, and he has reported feeling tired and stressed as a result. Despite recommendations to improve his fitness, he has not been able to reduce his weight significantly or make changes to his lifestyle.

Mr Collister has no known allergies and he contracted infectious mononucleosis in 2006.

It would be appreciated if you could assess Mr Collister's condition to confirm the preliminary diagnosis, and, if appropriate, recommend a management plan.

Yours sincerely,

Doctor

MEDICINE

PRACTICE TEST 2

To listen to the audio, visit
https://www.occupationalenglishtest.org/audio

LISTENING SUB-TEST – QUESTION PAPER

CANDIDATE NUMBER:

LAST NAME:

FIRST NAME:

MIDDLE NAMES:

PROFESSION:

VENUE:

TEST DATE:

Candidate details and photo will be printed here.

Passport Photo

CANDIDATE DECLARATION
By signing this, you agree not to disclose or use in any way (other than to take the test) or assist any other person to disclose or use any OET test or sub-test content. If you cheat or assist in any cheating, use any unfair practice, break any of the rules or regulations, or ignore any advice or information, you may be disqualified and your results may not be issued at the sole discretion of CBLA. CBLA also reserves its right to take further disciplinary action against you and to pursue any other remedies permitted by law. If a candidate is suspected of and investigated for malpractice, their personal details and details of the investigation may be passed to a third party where required.

CANDIDATE SIGNATURE: _____

TIME: APPROXIMATELY 40 MINUTES

INSTRUCTIONS TO CANDIDATES

DO NOT open this question paper until you are told to do so.

One mark will be granted for each correct answer.

Answer **ALL** questions. Marks are **NOT** deducted for incorrect answers.

At the end of the test, you will have two minutes to check your answers.

At the end of the test, hand in this **Question Paper**.

You must not remove OET material from the test room.

HOW TO ANSWER THE QUESTIONS

Part A: Write your answers on this **Question Paper** by filling in the blanks. **Example: Patient:** _Ray Sands_

Part B & Part C: Mark your answers on this **Question Paper** by filling in the circle using a 2B pencil. **Example:** Ⓐ Ⓑ Ⓒ

www.occupationalenglishtest.org
© Cambridge Boxhill Language Assessment – ABN 51 988 559 414
[CANDIDATE NO.] LISTENING QUESTION PAPER 01/12

PRACTICE TEST 2

Occupational English Test
Listening Test

This test has three parts. In each part you'll hear a number of different extracts. At the start of each extract, you'll hear this sound: --beep—

You'll have time to read the questions before you hear each extract and you'll hear each extract **ONCE ONLY**. Complete your answers as you listen.

At the end of the test you'll have two minutes to check your answers.

Part A

In this part of the test, you'll hear two different extracts. In each extract, a health professional is talking to a patient.

For **questions 1-24**, complete the notes with information you hear.

Now, look at the notes for extract one.

Extract 1: Questions 1-12

You hear a consultant endocrinologist talking to a patient called Sarah Croft. For **questions 1-12**, complete the notes with a word or short phrase.

You now have 30 seconds to look at the notes.

Patient	Sarah Croft
Medical history	• hypertension (recently worsened)
	• 3 years of corticosteroid treatment for **(1)** _____
General symptoms	
	• gradual weight gain, especially in stomach area
	• **(2)** _____ on face: embarrassing
	• visible **(3)** _____ between the shoulders
	• swollen ankles
	• excessive and constant **(4)** _____
	• backache
	• periods are **(5)** _____
	• extreme tiredness
Dermatological symptoms	
	• tendency to **(6)** _____
	• wounds slow to heal, **(7)** _____ on thighs
	• face appears red in colour, **(8)** _____ area on neck
	• recent development of **(9)** _____

Psychological symptoms

- mildly depressed
- scared by new experience of **(10)** _____
- feels constantly **(11)** _____
- intermittent cognitive difficulties

Recommended tests

- further blood tests
- **(12)** _____ test possibly

Extract 2: Questions 13-24

You hear an anaesthetist talking to a patient called Mary Wilcox prior to an operation. For **questions 13-24**, complete the notes with a word or short phrase.
You now have thirty seconds to look at the notes.

Patient   Mary Wilcox

Current medications

Reason for medication	Medication	Comments
High blood pressure	Thiazide	both taken this morning with **(14)** _____
	(13) _____	
Heart attack	**(15)** _____	taken this morning
	(16) _____	stopped taking this 7 days ago

Medical history
- went to GP two years ago feeling **(17)** _____ – heart attack subsequently diagnosed
- had two **(18)** _____ inserted

Present condition

- alright with **(19)** _____ and walking on the flat
- has swelling in one ankle following operation for **(20)** _____
- denies **(21)** _____
- reports some **(22)** _____ at night (responds to medication)

Concerns expressed

- **(23)** _____ following the procedure
- possible damage to crowns (both are **(24)** _____)

That is the end of Part A. Now look at Part B.

Part B

In this part of the test, you'll hear six different extracts. In each extract, you'll hear people talking in a different healthcare setting.

For **questions 25-30**, choose the answer (**A**, **B** or **C**) which fits best according to what you hear. You'll have time to read each question before you listen. Complete your answers as you listen.

Now look at question 25.

25. You hear two trainee doctors doing an activity at a staff training day.

   What does the activity give practice in?

   A   writing case notes

   B   prioritising patients

   C   dealing with consultants

26. You hear a radiographer talking to a patient about her MRI scan.

   What is he doing?

   A   clarifying the aim of the procedure

   B   dealing with her particular concerns

   C   explaining how the equipment works

27. You hear two nurses discussing an article in a nursing journal.

   What do they agree about it?

   A   It's likely to lead to changes in practice.

   B   It failed to reach any definite conclusion.

   C   It confirms what they were already thinking.

28. You hear two hospital managers talking about a time management course for staff.

   They think that few people have shown interest because

   A   there are so many alternatives on offer.

   B   they feel it's not relevant to them.

   C   it hasn't been publicised enough.

29. You hear an optometrist reporting on some research he's been doing.

   The aim of his research was

   A   to develop nanoparticles for transporting drugs all over the body.

   B   to find a way of treating infections caused by contact lenses.

   C   to use contact lenses to administer drugs over time.

30. You hear a consultant talking to a trainee about a patient's eye condition.

   What is the consultant doing?

   A   explaining why intervention may not be necessary

   B   suggesting the diagnosis is by no means certain

   C   describing a possible complication

That is the end of Part B. Now look at Part C.

Part C

In this part of the test, you'll hear two different extracts. In each extract, you'll hear health professionals talking about aspects of their work.

For **questions 31-42**, choose the answer (**A**, **B** or **C**) which fits best according to what you hear. Complete your answers as you listen.

Now look at extract one.

Extract 1: Questions 31-36

You hear an interview with a neurosurgeon called Dr Ian Marsh who specialises in the treatment of concussion in sport.

You now have 90 seconds to read **questions 31-36**.

31. Dr Marsh says that one aim of the new guidelines on concussion is

    A   to educate young sportspeople in how to avoid getting it.

    B   to correct some common misunderstandings about it.

    C   to provide a range of specialist advice about it.

32. Dr Marsh makes the point that someone who has suffered a concussion will

    A   be unconscious for varying amounts of time after the event.

    B   need a medical examination before doing any further exercise.

    C   have to take precautions to avoid the risk of symptoms recurring.

33. Dr Marsh says returning to sport too early after a concussion is dangerous because

    A   a subsequent episode can have a cumulative effect.

    B   there is a high risk of fatality in the event of a second one.

    C   the brains of younger people need time to return to normal size.

84   PRACTICE TEST 2

34. Dr Marsh suggests that the risk of sustaining a concussion in sports

   A   lies mainly in the choice of sports played.

   B   can be reduced by developing good playing technique.

   C   is greater when sports are played in less formal situations.

35. What is Dr Marsh's view about providing medical support for youth sports events?

   A   Some types of sport are risky enough to justify it.

   B   The organisers should be capable of dealing with any issues.

   C   Certain medical professionals should be encouraged to volunteer.

36. Dr Marsh thinks that developments in college football in the USA

   A   only really address an issue which is particular to that sport.

   B   are only likely to benefit the health of professional sports players.

   C   are a significant step forward in the prevention of concussion in all sports.

Now look at extract two.

Extract 2: Questions 37-42

You hear a presentation by a consultant cardiologist called Dr Pamela Skelton, who's talking about a research trial called SPRINT which investigated the effects of setting lower blood-pressure targets.

You now have 90 seconds to read **questions 37-42**.

37. Why was the SPRINT trial stopped before it was due to end?

    A   There were conclusive results earlier than expected.

    B   The high drop-out rate was likely to invalidate the data.

    C   Concerns were raised about possible effects on all participants.

38. A few participants aged over seventy-five left the trial because

    A   there was a negative impact on their daily life.

    B   they failed to take the required doses of medication.

    C   their health deteriorated due to pre-existing conditions.

39. A significant feature of measuring blood pressure in the trial was that

    A   the highest of three readings was recorded.

    B   the patient was alone when it was carried out.

    C   it was done manually by the participant at home.

40. How did the SPRINT trial differ from the earlier ACCORD study into blood pressure?

- (A) SPRINT had fewer participants.
- (B) SPRINT involved higher-risk patients.
- (C) SPRINT included patients with diabetes.

41. Dr Skelton's main reservation about the SPRINT trial is that

- (A) it ignores the wider implications of lowered BP.
- (B) its results go against the existing body of evidence.
- (C) it was unduly influenced by pharmaceutical companies.

42. What impact does Dr Skelton think the SPRINT trial will have in the future?

- (A) It will lead to universally applicable guidelines for BP levels.
- (B) Increased attention will be given to the effect of lifestyle on BP.
- (C) GPs will adopt a more active approach to lowering BP in the elderly.

That is the end of Part C.

You now have two minutes to check your answers.

END OF THE LISTENING TEST

READING SUB-TEST – TEXT BOOKLET: PART A

CANDIDATE NUMBER:
LAST NAME:
FIRST NAME:
MIDDLE NAMES:
PROFESSION:
VENUE:
TEST DATE:

Candidate details and photo will be printed here.

Passport Photo

CANDIDATE DECLARATION
By signing this, you agree not to disclose or use in any way (other than to take the test) or assist any other person to disclose or use any OET test or sub-test content. If you cheat or assist in any cheating, use any unfair practice, break any of the rules or regulations, or ignore any advice or information, you may be disqualified and your results may not be issued at the sole discretion of CBLA. CBLA also reserves its right to take further disciplinary action against you and to pursue any other remedies permitted by law. If a candidate is suspected of and investigated for malpractice, their personal details and details of the investigation may be passed to a third party where required.

CANDIDATE SIGNATURE: _____

INSTRUCTIONS TO CANDIDATES
You must **NOT** remove OET material from the test room.

www.occupationalenglishtest.org
© Cambridge Boxhill Language Assessment – ABN 51 988 559 414

[CANDIDATE NO.] READING TEXT BOOKLET PART A 01/04

Tetanus: Texts

Text A

Tetanus is a severe disease that can result in serious illness and death. Tetanus vaccination protects against the disease.

Tetanus (sometimes called lock-jaw) is a disease caused by the bacteria Clostridium tetani. Toxins made by the bacteria attack a person's nervous system. Although the disease is fairly uncommon, it can be fatal.

Early symptoms of tetanus include:

- Painful muscle contractions that begin in the jaw (lock jaw)
- Rigidity in neck, shoulder and back muscles
- Difficulty swallowing
- Violent generalized muscle spasms
- Convulsions
- Breathing difficulties

A person may have a fever and sometimes develop abnormal heart rhythms. Complications include pneumonia, broken bones (from the muscle spasms), respiratory failure and cardiac arrest.

There is no specific diagnostic laboratory test; diagnosis is made clinically. The spatula test is useful: touching the back of the pharynx with a spatula elicits a bite reflex in tetanus, instead of a gag reflex.

Text B

Tetanus Risk

Tetanus is an acute disease induced by the toxin tetanus bacilli, the spores of which are present in soil.

A TETANUS-PRONE WOUND IS:

- any wound or burn that requires surgical intervention that is delayed for > 6 hours
- any wound or burn at any interval after injury that shows one or more of the following characteristics:
  - a significant degree of tissue damage
  - puncture-type wound particularly where there has been contact with soil or organic matter which is likely to harbour tetanus organisms
- any wound from compound fractures
- any wound containing foreign bodies
- any wound or burn in patients who have systemic sepsis
- any bite wound
- any wound from tooth re-implantation

Intravenous drug users are at greater risk of tetanus. Every opportunity should be taken to ensure that they are fully protected against tetanus. Booster doses should be given if there is any doubt about their immunisation status.

Immunosuppressed patients may not be adequately protected against tetanus, despite having been fully immunised. They should be managed as if they were incompletely immunised.

Text C

Tetanus Immunisation following injuries

Thorough cleaning of the wound is essential irrespective of the immunisation history of the patient, and appropriate antibiotics should be prescribed.

Immunisation Status	Clean Wound	Tetanus-prone wound	
	Vaccine	Vaccine	Human Tetanus Immunoglobulin (HTIG)
Fully immunised[1]	Not required	Not required	Only if high risk[2]
Primary immunisation complete, boosters incomplete but up to date	Not required	Not required	Only if high risk[2]
Primary immunisation incomplete or boosters not up to date	Reinforcing dose and further doses to complete recommended schedule	Reinforcing dose and further doses to complete recommended schedule	Yes (opposite limb to vaccine)
Not immunised or immunisation status not known/uncertain[3]	Immediate dose of vaccine followed by completion of full 5-dose course	Immediate dose of vaccine followed by completion of full 5-dose course	Yes (opposite limb to vaccine)

Notes
1. has received total of 5 doses of vaccine at appropriate intervals
2. heavy contamination with material likely to contain tetanus spores and/or extensive devitalised tissue
3. immunosuppressed patients presenting with a tetanus-prone wound should always be managed as if they were incompletely immunised

Text D

Human Tetanus Immunoglobulin (HTIG)

Indications

- treatment of clinically suspected cases of tetanus
- prevention of tetanus in high-risk, tetanus-prone wounds

Dose

Available in 1ml ampoules containing 250IU

Prevention Dose	Treatment Dose
250 IU by IM injection[1] Or 500 IU by IM injection[1] if >24 hours since injury/risk of heavy contamination/burns	5,000 – 10,000 IU by IV infusion Or 150 IU/kg by IM injection[1] (given in multiple sites) if IV preparation unavailable

[1] Due to its viscosity, HTIG should be administered slowly, using a 23 gauge needle

Contraindications

- Confirmed anaphylactic reaction to tetanus containing vaccine
- Confirmed anaphylactic reaction to neomycin, streptomycin or polymyxin B

Adverse reactions

Local – pain, erythema, induration (Arthus-type reaction)

General – pyrexia, hypotonic-hyporesponsive episode, persistent crying

END OF PART A

THIS TEXT BOOKLET WILL BE COLLECTED

READING SUB-TEST – QUESTION PAPER: PART A

CANDIDATE NUMBER:

LAST NAME:

FIRST NAME:

MIDDLE NAMES:

PROFESSION:

VENUE:

TEST DATE:

Candidate details and photo will be printed here.

Passport Photo

CANDIDATE DECLARATION
By signing this, you agree not to disclose or use in any way (other than to take the test) or assist any other person to disclose or use any OET test or sub-test content. If you cheat or assist in any cheating, use any unfair practice, break any of the rules or regulations, or ignore any advice or information, you may be disqualified and your results may not be issued at the sole discretion of CBLA. CBLA also reserves its right to take further disciplinary action against you and to pursue any other remedies permitted by law. If a candidate is suspected of and investigated for malpractice, their personal details and details of the investigation may be passed to a third party where required.

CANDIDATE SIGNATURE: _____

TIME: 15 MINUTES

INSTRUCTIONS TO CANDIDATES

DO NOT open this **Question Paper** or the **Text Booklet** until you are told to do so.

Write your answers on the spaces provided on this **Question Paper.**

You must answer the questions within the 15-minute time limit.

One mark will be granted for each correct answer.

Answer **ALL** questions. Marks are **NOT** deducted for incorrect answers.

At the end of the 15 minutes, hand in this **Question Paper** and the **Text Booklet.**

DO NOT remove OET material from the test room.

www.occupationalenglishtest.org
© Cambridge Boxhill Language Assessment – ABN 51 988 559 414
[CANDIDATE NO.] READING QUESTION PAPER PART A 01/04

Part A

TIME: 15 minutes

- Look at the four texts, **A-D**, in the separate **Text Booklet**.
- For each question, **1-20**, look through the texts, **A-D**, to find the relevant information.
- Write your answers on the spaces provided in this **Question Paper**.
- Answer all the questions within the 15-minute time limit.
- Your answers should be correctly spelt.

Tetanus: Questions

Questions 1-6

For each question, **1-6**, decide which text (**A**, **B**, **C** or **D**) the information comes from.
You may use any letter more than once.

In which text can you find information about

1   the type of injuries that may lead to tetanus?   _____

2   signs that a patient may have tetanus?   _____

3   how to decide whether a tetanus vaccine is necessary?   _____

4   an alternative name for tetanus?   _____

5   possible side-effects of a particular tetanus medication?   _____

6   other conditions which are associated with tetanus?   _____

Questions 7-13

Complete each of the sentences, **7-13**, with a word or short phrase from one of the texts.
Each answer may include words, numbers or both.

Patients at increased risk of tetanus:

7   If a patient has been touching _____ or earth, they are more susceptible to tetanus.

8   Any _____ lodged in the site of an injury will increase the likelihood of tetanus.

9   Patients with _____ fractures are prone to tetanus.

10   Delaying surgery on an injury or burn by more than _____ increases the probability of tetanus.

11   If a burns patient has been diagnosed with _____ they are more liable to contract tetanus.

94   PRACTICE TEST 2

12 A patient who is _____ or a regular recreational drug user will be at greater risk of tetanus.

Management of tetanus-prone injuries:

13 Clean the wound thoroughly and prescribe _____ if necessary, followed by tetanus vaccine and HTIG as appropriate.

Questions 14-20

Answer each of the questions, **14-20**, with a word or short phrase from one of the texts. Each answer may include words, numbers or both.

14 Where will a patient suffering from tetanus first experience muscle contractions?

15 What can muscle spasms in tetanus patients sometimes lead to?

16 If you test for tetanus using a spatula, what type of reaction will confirm the condition?

17 How many times will you have to vaccinate a patient who needs a full course of tetanus vaccine?

18 What should you give a drug user if you're uncertain of their vaccination history?

19 What size of needle should you use to inject HTIG?

20 What might a patient who experienced an adverse reaction to HTIG be unable to stop doing?

END OF PART A
THIS QUESTION PAPER WILL BE COLLECTED

READING SUB-TEST – QUESTION PAPER: PARTS B & C

CANDIDATE NUMBER:

LAST NAME:

FIRST NAME:

MIDDLE NAMES:

PROFESSION:

VENUE:

TEST DATE:

Candidate details and photo will be printed here.

Passport Photo

CANDIDATE DECLARATION
By signing this, you agree not to disclose or use in any way (other than to take the test) or assist any other person to disclose or use any OET test or sub-test content. If you cheat or assist in any cheating, use any unfair practice, break any of the rules or regulations, or ignore any advice or information, you may be disqualified and your results may not be issued at the sole discretion of CBLA. CBLA also reserves its right to take further disciplinary action against you and to pursue any other remedies permitted by law. If a candidate is suspected of and investigated for malpractice, their personal details and details of the investigation may be passed to a third party where required.

CANDIDATE SIGNATURE: _____

TIME: 45 MINUTES

INSTRUCTIONS TO CANDIDATES

DO NOT open this **Question Paper** until you are told to do so.

One mark will be granted for each correct answer.

Answer **ALL** questions. Marks are **NOT** deducted for incorrect answers.

At the end of the test, hand in this **Question Paper**.

HOW TO ANSWER THE QUESTIONS:

Mark your answers on this **Question Paper** by filling in the circle using a 2B pencil. **Example:** Ⓐ Ⓑ Ⓒ

www.occupationalenglishtest.org
© Cambridge Boxhill Language Assessment – ABN 51 988 559 414
[CANDIDATE NO.] READING QUESTION PAPER PARTS B & C 01/16

Part B

In this part of the test, there are six short extracts relating to the work of health professionals. For **questions 1-6**, choose answer (**A**, **B** or **C**) which you think fits best according to the text.

1. Nursing staff can remove a dressing if

    (A) a member of the surgical team is present.

    (B) there is severe leakage from the wound.

    (C) they believe that the wound has healed.

> **Post-operative dressings**
>
> Dressings are an important component of post-operative wound management. Any dressings applied during surgery have been done in sterile conditions and should ideally be left in place, as stipulated by the surgical team. It is acceptable for initial dressings to be removed prematurely in order to have the wound reviewed and, in certain situations, apply a new dressing. These situations include when the dressing is no longer serving its purpose (i.e. dressing falling off, excessive exudate soaking through the dressing and resulting in a suboptimal wound healing environment) or when a wound complication is suspected.

2. As explained in the protocol, the position of the RUM container will ideally

- (A) encourage participation in the scheme.
- (B) emphasise the value of recycling.
- (C) facilitate public access to it.

Unwanted medicine: pharmacy collection protocol

A Returned Unwanted Medicine (RUM) Project approved container will be delivered by the wholesaler to the participating pharmacy.

The container is to be kept in a section of the dispensary or in a room or enclosure in the pharmacy to which the public does not have access. The container may be placed in a visible position, but out of reach of the public, as this will reinforce the message that unwanted prescription drugs can be returned to the pharmacy and that the returned medicines will not be recycled.

Needles, other sharps and liquid cytotoxic products should not be placed in the container, but in one specifically designed for such waste.

3. The report mentioned in the memo suggests that

   (A) data about patient errors may be incomplete.

   (B) errors by hospital staff can often go unreported.

   (C) errors in prescriptions pose the greatest threat to patients.

Memo: Report on oral anti-cancer medications
Nurse Unit Managers are directed to review their systems for the administration of oral anti-cancer drugs, and the reporting of drug errors. Serious concerns have been raised in a recent report drawing on a national survey of pharmacists. Please note the following paragraph quoted from the report: > Incorrect doses of oral anti-cancer medicines can have fatal consequences. Over the previous four years, there were three deaths and 400 patient safety issues involving oral anti-cancer medicines. Half of the reports concerned the wrong dosage, frequency, quantity or duration of oral anti-cancer treatment. Of further concern is that errors on the part of patients may be under-reported. In light of these reports, there is clearly a need for improved systems covering the management of patients receiving oral therapies.

4. What point does the training manual make about anaesthesia workstations?

- A Parts of the equipment have been shown to be vulnerable to failure.
- B There are several ways of ensuring that the ventilator is working effectively.
- C Monitoring by health professionals is a reliable way to maintain patient safety.

Anaesthesia Workstations

Studies on safety in anaesthesia have documented that human vigilance alone is inadequate to ensure patient safety and have underscored the importance of monitoring devices. These findings are reflected in improved standards for equipment design, guidelines for patient monitoring and reduced malpractice premiums for the use of capnography and pulse oximetry during anaesthesia. Anaesthesia workstations integrate ventilator technology with patient monitors and alarms to help prevent patient injury in the unlikely event of a ventilator failure. Furthermore, since the reservoir bag is part of the circuit during mechanical ventilation, the visible movement of the reservoir bag is confirmation that the ventilator is functioning.

5. In cases of snakebite, the flying doctor should be aware of

   (A) where to access specific antivenoms.

   (B) the appropriate method for wound cleaning.

   (C) the patients most likely to suffer complications.

Memo to Flying Doctor staff: Antivenoms for snakebite
Before starting treatment: • Do not wash the snakebite site. • If possible, determine the type of snake by using a 'snake-venom detection kit' to test a bite site swab or, in systemic envenoming, the person's urine. If venom detection is not available or has proved negative, seek advice from a poisons information centre. • Testing blood for venom is not reliable. • Assess the degree of envenoming; not all confirmed snakebites will result in systemic envenoming; risk varies with the species of snake. • People with pre-existing renal, hepatic, cardiac or respiratory impairment and those taking anticoagulant or antiplatelet drugs may have an increased risk of serious outcome from snakebite. Children are also especially at increased risk of severe envenoming because of smaller body mass and the likelihood of physical activity immediately after a bite.

6. What was the purpose of the BMTEC forum?

   (A) to propose a new way of carrying out cleaning audits

   (B) to draw conclusions from the results of cleaning audits

   (C) to encourage more groups to undertake cleaning audits

Cleaning Audits
Three rounds of environmental cleaning audits were completed in 2013-2014. Key personnel in each facility were surveyed to assess the understanding of environmental cleaning from the perspective of the nurse unit manager, environmental services manager and the director of clinical governance. Each facility received a report about their environmental cleaning audits and lessons learned from the surveys. Data from the 15 units were also provided to each facility for comparison purposes.
The knowledge and experiences from the audits were shared at the BMTEC Forum in August 2014. This forum allowed environmental services managers, cleaners, nurses and clinical governance to discuss the application of the standards and promote new and improved cleaning practice. The second day of the forum focused on auditor training and technique with the view of enhancing internal environmental cleaning auditing by the participating groups.

Part C

In this part of the test, there are two texts about different aspects of healthcare. For **questions 7-22**, choose the answer (**A**, **B**, **C** or **D**) which you think fits best according to the text.

Text 1: Does homeopathy 'work'?

For many, homeopathy is simply unscientific, but regular users hold a very different view.

Homeopathy works by giving patients very dilute substances that, in larger doses, would cause the very symptoms that need curing. Taking small doses of these substances – derived from plants, animals or minerals – strengthens the body's ability to heal and increases resistance to illness or infection. Or that is the theory. The debate about its effectiveness is nothing new. Recently, Australia's National Health and Medical Research Council (NHMRC) released a paper which found there were 'no health conditions for which there was reliable evidence that homeopathy was effective'. This echoed a report from the UK House of Commons which said that the evidence failed to show a 'credible physiological mode of action' for homeopathic products, and that what data were available showed homeopathic products to be no better than placebo. Yet Australians spend at least $11 million per year on homeopathy.

So what's going on? If Australians – and citizens of many other nations around the world – are voting with their wallets, does this mean homeopathy must be doing something right? 'For me, the crux of the debate is a disconnect between how the scientific and medical community view homeopathy, and what many in the wider community are getting out of it,' says Professor Alex Broom of the University of Queensland. 'The really interesting question is how can we possibly have something that people think works, when to all intents and purposes, from a scientific perspective, it doesn't?'

Part of homeopathy's appeal may lie in the nature of the patient-practitioner consultation. In contrast to a typical 15-minute GP consultation, a first homeopathy consultation might take an hour and a half. 'We don't just look at an individual symptom in isolation. For us, that symptom is part of someone's overall health condition,' says Greg Cope, spokesman for the Australian Homeopathic Association. 'Often we'll have a consultation with someone and find details their GP simply didn't have time to.' Writer Johanna Ashmore is a case in point. She sees her homeopath for a one-hour monthly consultation. 'I feel, if I go and say I've got this health concern, she's going to treat my body to fight it rather than just treat the symptom.'

Most people visit a homeopath after having received a diagnosis from a 'mainstream' practitioner, often because they want an alternative choice to medication, says Greg Cope. 'Generally speaking, for a homeopath, their preference is if someone has a diagnosis from a medical practitioner before starting homeopathic treatment, so it's rare for someone to come and see us with an undiagnosed condition and certainly if they do come undiagnosed, we'd want to refer them on and get that medical evaluation before starting a course of treatment,' he says.

Given that homeopathic medicines are by their very nature incredibly dilute – and, some might argue, diluted beyond all hope of efficacy – they are unlikely to cause any adverse effects, so where's the harm? Professor Paul Glasziou, chair of the NHMRC's Homeopathy Working Committee, says that while financial cost is one harm, potentially more harmful are the non-financial costs associated with missing out on effective treatments. 'If it's just a cold, I'm not too worried. But if it's for a serious illness, you may not be taking disease-modifying treatments, and most worrying is things like HIV which affect not only you, but people around you,' says Glasziou. This is a particular concern with homeopathic vaccines, he says, which jeopardise the 'herd immunity' – the immunity of a significant proportion of the population – which is crucial in containing outbreaks of vaccine-preventable diseases.

The question of a placebo effect inevitably arises, as studies repeatedly seem to suggest that whatever benefits are being derived from homeopathy are more a product of patient faith rather than of any active ingredient of the medications. However, Greg Cope dismisses this argument, pointing out that homeopathy appears to benefit even the sceptics: 'We might see kids first, then perhaps Mum and after a couple of years, Dad will follow and, even though he's only there reluctantly, we get **wonderful outcomes**. This cannot be explained simply by the placebo effect.' As a patient, Johanna Ashmore is aware scientific research does little to support homeopathy but can still see its benefits. 'If seeing my homeopath each month improves my health, I'm happy. I don't care how it works, even if it's all in the mind – I just know that it does.'

But if so many people around the world are placing their faith in homeopathy, despite the evidence against it, Broom questions why homeopathy seeks scientific validation. The problem, as he sees it, lies in the fact that 'if you're going to dance with conventional medicine and say "we want to be proven to be effective in dealing with discrete physiological conditions", then you indeed do have to show efficacy. In my view **this** is not about broader credibility per se, it's about scientific and medical credibility – there's actually quite a lot of cultural credibility surrounding homeopathy within the community but that's not replicated in the scientific literature.'

Text 1: Questions 7-14

7. The two reports mentioned in the first paragraph both concluded that homeopathy

   A   could be harmful if not used appropriately.

   B   merely works on the same basis as the placebo effect.

   C   lacks any form of convincing proof of its value as a treatment.

   D   would require further investigation before it was fully understood.

8. When commenting on the popularity of homeopathy, Professor Broom shows his

   A   surprise at people's willingness to put their trust in it.

   B   frustration at scientists' inability to explain their views on it.

   C   acceptance of the view that the subject may merit further study.

   D   concern over the risks people face when receiving such treatment.

9. Johanna Ashmore's views on homeopathy highlight

   A   how practitioners put their patients at ease.

   B   the key attraction of the approach for patients.

   C   how it suits patients with a range of health problems.

   D   the opportunities to improve patient care which GPs miss.

10. In the fourth paragraph, it is suggested that visits to homeopaths

    A   occasionally depend on a referral from a mainstream doctor.

    B   frequently result from a patient's treatment preferences.

    C   should be preceded by a visit to a relevant specialist.

    D   often reveal previously overlooked medical problems.

11. What particularly concerns Professor Glasziou?

- (A) the risks to patients of relying on homeopathic vaccinations
- (B) the mistaken view that homeopathic treatments can only do good
- (C) the way that homeopathic remedies endanger more than just the user
- (D) the ineffectiveness of homeopathic remedies against even minor illnesses

12. Greg Cope uses the expression '**wonderful outcomes**' to underline

- (A) the ability of homeopathy to defy its scientific critics.
- (B) the value of his patients' belief in the whole process.
- (C) the claim that he has solid proof that homeopathy works.
- (D) the way positive results can be achieved despite people's doubts.

13. From the comments quoted in the sixth paragraph, it is clear that Johanna Ashmore is

- (A) prepared to accept that homeopathy may depend on psychological factors.
- (B) happy to admit that she was uncertain at first about proceeding.
- (C) sceptical about the evidence against homeopathic remedies.
- (D) confident that research will eventually validate homeopathy.

14. What does the word '**this**' in the final paragraph refer to?

- (A) the continuing inability of homeopathy to gain scientific credibility
- (B) the suggestion that the scientific credibility of homeopathy is in doubt
- (C) the idea that there is no need to pursue scientific acceptance for homeopathy
- (D) the motivation behind the desire for homeopathy to gain scientific acceptance

Text 2: Brain-controlled prosthetics

Paralysed from the neck down by a stroke, Cathy Hutchinson stared fixedly at a drinking straw in a bottle on the table in front of her. A cable rose from the top of her head, connecting her to a robot arm, but her gaze never wavered as she mentally guided the robot arm, which was opposite her, to close its grippers around the bottle, then slowly lift the vessel towards her mouth. Only when she finally managed to take a sip did her face relax. This example illustrates the strides being taken in brain-controlled prosthetics. But Hutchinson's focused stare also illustrates the one crucial feature still missing from prosthetics. Her eyes could tell her where the arm was, but she couldn't feel what it was doing.

Prosthetics researchers are now trying to create prosthetics that can 'feel'. It's a **daunting** task: the researchers have managed to read signals from the brain; now they must write information into the nervous system. Touch encompasses a complicated mix of information – everything from the soft prickliness of wool to the slipping of a sweaty soft-drink can. The sensations arise from a host of receptors in the skin, which detect texture, vibration, pain, temperature and shape, as well as from receptors in the muscles, joints and tendons that contribute to 'proprioception' – the sense of where a limb is in space. Prosthetics are being outfitted with sensors that can gather many of these sensations, but the challenge is to get the resulting signals flowing to the correct part of the brain.

For people who have had limbs amputated, the obvious way to achieve that is to route the signals into the remaining nerves in the stump, the part of the limb left after amputation. Ken Horch, a neuroprosthetics researcher, has done just that by threading electrodes into the nerves in stumps then stimulating them with a tiny current, so that patients felt like their fingers were moving or being touched. The technique can even allow patients to distinguish basic features of objects: a man who had lost his lower arms was able to determine the difference between blocks made of wood or foam rubber by using a sensor-equipped prosthetic hand. He correctly identified the objects' size and softness more than twice as often as would have been expected by chance. Information about force and finger position was delivered from the prosthetic to a computer, which prompted stimulation of electrodes implanted in his upper-arm nerves.

As promising as this result was, researchers will probably need to stimulate hundreds or thousands of nerve fibres to create complex sensations, and they'll need to keep the devices working for many years if they are to minimise the number of surgeries required to replace them as they wear out. To get around this, some researchers are instead trying to give patients sensory feedback by touching their skin. The technique was discovered by accident by researcher Todd Kuiken. The idea was to rewire arm nerves that used to serve the hand, for example, to muscles in other parts of the body. When the patient thought about closing his or her hand, the newly targeted muscle would contract and generate an electric signal, driving movement of the prosthetic.

However, this technique won't work for stroke patients like Cathy Hutchinson. So some researchers are skipping directly to the brain. In principle, this should be straightforward. Because signals from specific parts of the body go to specific parts of the brain, scientists should be able to create sensations of touch or proprioception in the limb by directly activating the neurons that normally receive those signals. However, with electrical stimulation, all neurons close to the electrode's tip are activated indiscriminately, so 'even if I had the sharpest needle in the Universe, that could create unintended effects', says Arto Nurmikko, a neuroengineer. For example, an attempt to create sensation in one finger might produce sensation in other parts of the hand as well, he says.

Nurmikko and other researchers are therefore using light, in place of electricity, to activate highly specific groups of neurons and recreate a sense of touch. They trained a monkey to remove its hand from a pad when it vibrated. When the team then stimulated the part of its brain that receives tactile information from the hand with a light source implanted in its skull, the monkey lifted its hand off the pad about 90% of the time. The use of such techniques in humans is still probably 10–20 years away, but it is a promising strategy.

Even if such techniques can be made to work, it's unclear how closely they will approximate natural sensations. Tingles, pokes and vibrations are still **a far cry from** the complicated sensations that we feel when closing a hand over an apple, or running a finger along a table's edge. But patients don't need a perfect sense of touch, says Douglas Weber, a bioengineer. Simply having enough feedback to improve their control of grasp could help people to perform tasks such as picking up a glass of water, he explains. He goes on to say that patients who wear cochlear implants, for example, are often happy to regain enough hearing to hold a phone conversation, even if they're still unable to distinguish musical subtleties.

Text 2: Questions 15-22

15. What do we learn about the experiment Cathy Hutchinson took part in?

    A   It required intense concentration.

    B   It failed to achieve what it had set out to do.

    C   It could be done more quickly given practice.

    D   It was the first time that it had been attempted.

16. The task facing researchers is described as '**daunting**' because

    A   signals from the brain can be misunderstood.

    B   it is hard to link muscle receptors with each other.

    C   some aspects of touch are too difficult to reproduce.

    D   the connections between sensors and the brain need to be exact.

17. What is said about the experiment done on the patient in the third paragraph?

    A   There was statistical evidence that it was successful.

    B   It enabled the patient to have a wide range of feeling.

    C   Its success depended on when amputation had taken place.

    D   It required the use of a specially developed computer program.

18. What drawback does the writer mention in the fourth paragraph?

    A   The devices have a high failure rate.

    B   Patients might have to undergo too many operations.

    C   It would only be possible to create rather simple sensations.

    D   The research into the new technique hasn't been rigorous enough.

PRACTICE TEST 2   109

19. What point is made in the fifth paragraph?

   A Severed nerves may be able to be reconnected.

   B More research needs to be done on stroke victims.

   C Scientists' previous ideas about the brain have been overturned.

   D It is difficult for scientists to pinpoint precise areas with an electrode.

20. What do we learn about the experiment that made use of light?

   A It can easily be replicated in humans.

   B It worked as well as could be expected.

   C It may have more potential than electrical stimulation.

   D It required more complex surgery than previous experiments.

21. In the final paragraph, the writer uses the phrase '**a far cry from**' to underline

   A how much more there is to achieve.

   B how complex experiments have become.

   C the need to reduce people's expectations.

   D the differences between types of artificial sensation.

22. Why does Weber give the example of a cochlear implant?

   A to underline the need for a similar breakthrough in prosthetics

   B to illustrate the fact that some sensation is better than none

   C to highlight the advances made in other areas of medicine

   D to demonstrate the ability of the body to relearn skills

END OF READING TEST
THIS BOOKLET WILL BE COLLECTED

WRITING SUB-TEST – TEST BOOKLET

CANDIDATE NUMBER:

LAST NAME:

FIRST NAME:

MIDDLE NAMES:

PROFESSION:

VENUE:

TEST DATE:

Candidate details and photo will be printed here.

Passport Photo

CANDIDATE DECLARATION

By signing this, you agree not to disclose or use in any way (other than to take the test) or assist any other person to disclose or use any OET test or sub-test content. If you cheat or assist in any cheating, use any unfair practice, break any of the rules or regulations, or ignore any advice or information, you may be disqualified and your results may not be issued at the sole discretion of CBLA. CBLA also reserves its right to take further disciplinary action against you and to pursue any other remedies permitted by law. If a candidate is suspected of and investigated for malpractice, their personal details and details of the investigation may be passed to a third party where required.

CANDIDATE SIGNATURE: _____

INSTRUCTIONS TO CANDIDATES

You must write your answer for the Writing sub-test in the **Writing Answer Booklet**.

You must **NOT** remove OET material from the test room.

www.occupationalenglishtest.org
© Cambridge Boxhill Language Assessment – ABN 51 988 559 414

[CANDIDATE NO.] WRITING SUB-TEST TEST BOOKLET 01/04

OCCUPATIONAL ENGLISH TEST

WRITING SUB-TEST: **MEDICINE**

TIME ALLOWED: **READING TIME: 5 MINUTES**
WRITING TIME: 40 MINUTES

Read the case notes below and complete the writing task which follows.

Notes:

You are a doctor at Stillwater Private Practice. You are examining a 70-year-old woman who believes she has worsening arthritis.

Patient details

Name: Mrs Carol Potter

DOB: 30.12.1947

Address: 21 Gumtree Road
Stillwater

Medical history:
- 2008 Osteoarthritis (OA) – mostly of hands & knees
- 2015 Hypertension (HT) – well controlled
- 2016 Skin cancer removed
- 2016 Insomnia – 2 years, intermittent
  Urinary tract infections (UTIs) – intermittent

Medications:
Ramipril 5mg daily
Panadol Osteo (extended release paracetamol) 2 tablets t.d.s.
Temazepam 10mg nocte p.r.n.

Family history: Mother – breast cancer

Social background: Administrative assistant (retired)

Presenting complaint: ↑ Pain in L knee with walking for last 12 months. Now quite severe – not relieved by regular Panadol Osteo. Pain can even occur at rest after a long walk

Treatment record
23.02.18

Subjective:
No joint swelling/redness
No recent injury to knee
R knee – some pain on walking, not nearly as bad as L knee

On examination:
Evidence of ↓ ROM of L knee due to pain
No swelling
Tender to pressure along joint

Treatment:
Referral for X-ray of L knee, blood tests
Review appointment to discuss results tomorrow
Prescribe pain relief – naproxen 250mg b.d.

24.02.18

Test results:
- X-ray: Evidence of severe OA in L knee – osteophytes and loss of joint space
  Patella appears normal
  No evidence of fractures
- Blood: FBE, UEC (normal)

Assessment: Likely worsening OA

Treatment: Arrange physiotherapy
↑Analgesia
Referral for surgical consultation – ? knee joint replacement

Writing Task:

Using the information given in the case notes, write a letter of referral to Dr Waters, a surgeon at Stillwater Private Hospital, for a surgical consultation. Address the letter to Dr Leigh Waters, Surgeon, Stillwater Private Hospital, 54 Main Street, Stillwater.

In your answer:
- **Expand the relevant notes into complete sentences**
- **Do not use note form**
- **Use letter format**

The body of the letter should be approximately 180–200 words.

WRITING SUB-TEST – ANSWER BOOKLET

CANDIDATE NUMBER:

LAST NAME:

FIRST NAME:

MIDDLE NAMES:

PROFESSION:

VENUE:

TEST DATE:

Candidate details and photo will be printed here.

Passport Photo

CANDIDATE DECLARATION

By signing this, you agree not to disclose or use in any way (other than to take the test) or assist any other person to disclose or use any OET test or sub-test content. If you cheat or assist in any cheating, use any unfair practice, break any of the rules or regulations, or ignore any advice or information, you may be disqualified and your results may not be issued at the sole discretion of CBLA. CBLA also reserves its right to take further disciplinary action against you and to pursue any other remedies permitted by law. If a candidate is suspected of and investigated for malpractice, their personal details and details of the investigation may be passed to a third party where required.

CANDIDATE SIGNATURE: _____

TIME ALLOWED
READING TIME: 5 MINUTES
WRITING TIME: 40 MINUTES

INSTRUCTIONS TO CANDIDATES

1. **Reading time: 5 minutes**
   During this time you may study the writing task and notes. You **MUST NOT** write, highlight, underline or make any notes.

2. **Writing time: 40 minutes**

3. Use the back page for notes and rough draft only. Notes and rough draft will **NOT** be marked.

   Please write your answer clearly on page 1 and page 2.

   Cross out anything you **DO NOT** want the examiner to consider.

4. You must write your answer for the Writing sub-test in this **Answer Booklet** using **pen or pencil**.

5. You must **NOT** remove OET material from the test room.

www.occupationalenglishtest.org
© Cambridge Boxhill Language Assessment – ABN 51 988 559 414

[CANDIDATE NO.] WRITING SUB-TEST ANSWER BOOKLET 01/04

Please record your answer on this page.

(Only answers on Page 1 and Page 2 will be marked.)

OET Writing sub-test – Answer booklet   1

[CANDIDATE NO.] WRITING SUB-TEST - ANSWER BOOKLET 02/04

Please record your answer on this page.

(Only answers on Page 1 and Page 2 will be marked.)

OET Writing sub-test – Answer booklet 2

[CANDIDATE NO.] WRITING SUB-TEST - ANSWER BOOKLET 03/04

Space for notes and rough draft. Only your answers on Page 1 and Page 2 will be marked.

SPEAKING SUB-TEST

CANDIDATE NUMBER:

LAST NAME:

FIRST NAME:

MIDDLE NAMES:

PROFESSION: Your details and photo will be printed here.

VENUE:

TEST DATE:

Passport Photo

CANDIDATE DECLARATION
By signing this, you agree not to disclose or use in any way (other than to take the test) or assist any other person to disclose or use any OET test or sub-test content. If you cheat or assist in any cheating, use any unfair practice, break any of the rules or regulations, or ignore any advice or information, you may be disqualified and your results may not be issued at the sole discretion of CBLA. CBLA also reserves its right to take further disciplinary action against you and to pursue any other remedies permitted by law. If a candidate is suspected of and investigated for malpractice, their personal details and details of the investigation may be passed to a third party where required.

CANDIDATE SIGNATURE: _____

INSTRUCTION TO CANDIDATES
Please confirm with the Interlocutor that your roleplay card number and colour match the Interlocutor card before you begin.

Interlocutor to complete only

ID No: _____ Passport: ☐ National ID: ☐ Alternative ID approved: ☐

Speaking sub-test:

ID document sighted? ☐   Photo match? ☐   Signature match? ☐   Did not attend? ☐

Interlocutor name: _____

Interlocutor signature: _____

www.occupationalenglishtest.org
© Cambridge Boxhill Language Assessment – ABN 51 988 559 414
[CANDIDATE NO.] SPEAKING SUB-TEST 01/04

OET Sample role-play

ROLEPLAYER CARD NO. 1 — MEDICINE

SETTING Suburban General Practice

PATIENT You are a new patient to this practice. Following a week of epigastric pain (in the stomach and abdominal area), your doctor ordered a barium meal test for you. You have come back for the result. You are worried about the possibility of cancer. You had a similar episode of pain five years ago but took the prescribed anti-ulcer tablets for only two weeks.

TASK
- Express your anxiety about the condition. Could you have prevented the current episode of illness by having completed a longer course of treatment five years ago?
- Insist on knowing what a gastroscopy involves. You don't like the sound of it at all.
- Be difficult to reassure. You want to know all the possible causes of this pain, including cancer or other non-malignant causes.

© Cambridge Boxhill Language Assessment   Sample role-play

OET Sample role-play

CANDIDATE CARD NO. 1 — MEDICINE

SETTING Suburban General Practice

DOCTOR The patient has a recurrence of epigastric pain. The barium meal which you ordered shows an ulcer on the lesser curve of the stomach which may be malignant. He/she is a new patient to your practice and you have no details of previous epigastric pain.

TASK
- Explain the findings to the patient and the possibility of malignancy.
- Question the patient about previous episodes of epigastric pain.
- Advise that you will need to refer him/her urgently for a gastroscopy for a definite diagnosis. Explain the procedure as simply as possible.
- Find out what information about the condition the patient wants now. Try to reassure the patient by mentioning other possible, non-malignant causes (e.g., ulcer, indigestion, etc.).

© Cambridge Boxhill Language Assessment   Sample role-play

OET Sample role-play

ROLEPLAYER CARD NO. 2   **MEDICINE**

SETTING   Suburban Clinic

PARENT   You are the parent of a young child who suffers from eczema (a skin condition). You have brought the child to the doctor because you are worried about the condition and what will happen in the future. You have heard a theory that eczema is related to food allergies and you are inclined to believe it.

TASK

- When asked, explain that you want the doctor to explain exactly what eczema is and if the child will grow out of it.

- Discuss the theory of food allergies with the doctor.

- Challenge the doctor if he/she is inclined to dismiss this theory.

- Finally agree to listen to the doctor's advice on managing the condition.

© Cambridge Boxhill Language Assessment   Sample role-play

OET Sample role-play

CANDIDATE CARD NO. 2   **MEDICINE**

SETTING   Suburban Clinic

DOCTOR   A worried parent has brought his/her young child, who suffers from eczema, to see you.

TASK

- Find out what the parent wants to know about eczema.

- Explain the condition, and talk about the prognosis, (e.g., it is connected with inherited sensitive skin, it can be controlled but not cured, the child is likely to grow out of it, etc.).

- Answer the parent's question about any possible relationship between eczema and food allergies.

- Give advice on management of the condition. Advise the parent to make sure the child avoids things that will irritate the skin (e.g., most soaps, wool next to the skin, scratching and rubbing the skin, etc.).

© Cambridge Boxhill Language Assessment   Sample role-play

Listening sub-test
ANSWER KEY – Parts A, B & C

LISTENING SUB-TEST – ANSWER KEY

PART A: QUESTIONS 1-12

1 asthma

2 hair (growth)

3 hump

4 sweating / perspiration / diaphoresis

5 (so) infrequent (now)

6 (easily) bruise

7 stretch marks / striae

8 dark / darkened

9 acne (vulgaris)

10 mood swings

11 irritable

12 saliva

PART A: QUESTIONS 13-24

13 lisinopril

14 (some) water

15 aspirin

16 clopidogrel

17 (a bit) breathless

18 stents

19 (going up/going down/up and down) stairs

20 varicose veins

21 (having) palpitations

22 heartburn / (acid) reflux

23 pain

24 central incisors

LISTENING SUB-TEST – ANSWER KEY

PART B: QUESTIONS 25-30

25	B	prioritising patients
26	B	dealing with her particular concerns
27	A	It's likely to lead to changes in practice.
28	B	they feel it's not relevant to them.
29	C	to use contact lenses to administer drugs over time.
30	A	explaining why intervention may not be necessary

PART C: QUESTIONS 31-36

31	C	to provide a range of specialist advice about it.
32	C	have to take precautions to avoid the risk of symptoms recurring.
33	A	a subsequent episode can have a cumulative effect.
34	A	lies mainly in the choice of sports played.
35	B	The organisers should be capable of dealing with any issues.
36	A	only really address an issue which is particular to that sport.

PART C: QUESTIONS 37-42

37	A	There were conclusive results earlier than expected.
38	C	their health deteriorated due to pre-existing conditions.
39	B	the patient was alone when it was carried out.
40	B	SPRINT involved higher-risk patients.
41	B	its results go against the existing body of evidence.
42	C	GPs will adopt a more active approach to lowering BP in the elderly.

END OF KEY

Listening sub-test
Audio Script – Practice test 2

OCCUPATIONAL ENGLISH TEST. PRACTICE TEST 2. LISTENING TEST.

This test has three parts. In each part you'll hear a number of different extracts. At the start of each extract, you'll hear this sound: ---***---.

You'll have time to read the questions before you hear each extract and you'll hear each extract ONCE only. Complete your answers as you listen.

At the end of the test, you'll have two minutes to check your answers.

Part A. In this part of the test, you'll hear two different extracts. In each extract, a health professional is talking to a patient. For questions 1 to 24, complete the notes with information you hear. Now, look at the notes for extract one.

PAUSE: 5 SECONDS
Extract one. Questions 1 to 12.

You hear a consultant endocrinologist talking to a patient called Sarah Croft. For questions 1 to 12, complete the notes with a word or short phrase. You now have thirty seconds to look at the notes.

PAUSE: 30 SECONDS
---***---

M: Good morning, Mrs Croft. I see your GP has referred you to me ...

F: Yes.

M: OK ... I've got some notes here with his referral letter, but it'd be helpful if you could tell me in your own words the sort of problems you've been experiencing?

F: OK, well, I've had high blood pressure for several years, but these last few months...that's tending to get worse. I've been on corticosteroids too these last three years or so, and that's a result of the fact that I've suffered from asthma since my teens.

M: I see. But I understand you've developed several other problems recently?

F: Oh yeah – as you can see, my stomach is huge – I've put on a lot of weight and it seems to be concentrated there. And, oh dear, I don't know what's happened to my face! All this hair which has appeared – it's...so embarrassing. And something else which I didn't notice at first, but which other people have pointed out to me – here, see? In between my shoulders, ah yeah, is this, well, I can only describe it as a hump. That really bothers me too.

M: Yes – I can see, erm...

F: And look at my ankles... they're swollen too. Something else which has got really bad is that I'm always sweating so much – even in cold weather. No amount of anti-perspirant seems to help.

M: That must be difficult. Erm, and any aches or pains?

F: Well, my...my back tends to ache a bit, but I take ibuprofen which helps. My periods used to be painful in the past, but, to be honest, they're so infrequent now that the pain really isn't a problem any more. I often feel tired though, in fact...like really tired.

M: And what about your skin?

F: Oh yeah… it seems to bruise at the slightest thing. And I've noticed that if I get a cut or a scratch or something, it takes ages to heal. And something else I've spotted on my thighs, see here…is these stretch marks. Ah yes, they're quite noticeable because they're a real purple colour. My face has changed too – I used to have quite pale skin, but, as you can see it's quite red now. And it looks, well, puffy – I mean it never used to look like that.

M: OK… so there's been quite a change.

F: Oh, definitely. And if you look, here, on my neck – the skin's gone dark. Really odd. I don't know what's happening – and, though I never really had it before, I've now got acne into the bargain!

M: Ahh tt must all be distressing. I…I can appreciate that this is having an effect on you. Erm, have you noticed your general mood changing at all?

F: Well, it's enough to get anyone down really – and, yes, I do feel a bit depressed. But the frightening thing is that I've started getting mood swings. I've never had them before. I mean, one minute I'm laughing and the next I'm crying – and.. and I don't know why. It's quite alarming.

M: Anything else?

F: Well I confess I feel, well…irritable all the time. Everything seems to get on my nerves! And I can't seem to concentrate like I used to, you know – I find it hard sometimes to do stuff in my head like working out a sum, or remembering names and things. I… I just hope that you can help find out what's wrong with me.

M: Well, I'm sure we will. Now, I see you've already had some blood tests, but I'll need to do one or two more. You've had a urine test to look at your blood sugar, so I probably won't need to repeat that. We may do a saliva test, depending on the bloods.

F: OK, I see. And how long will everything take, I mean before we know what's causing the problems?

M: Well, I'm afraid it can all take some time as diagnosis can be quite complicated and we may need to (FADE)

PAUSE: 10 SECONDS
Extract two. Questions 13 to 24.

You hear an anaesthetist talking to a patient called Mary Wilcox prior to an operation. For questions 13 to 24, complete the notes with a word or short phrase. You now have thirty seconds to look at the notes.

PAUSE: 30 SECONDS
---***---

M   So, Mrs. Wilcox, you tell me you've had high blood pressure, so are you taking any medications for that?

F   Yes, erm… a blue one and a white one

M   And do you know the names of the tablets?

F   Yes, so one's thiazide.

M   OK

F   and the other one's lisinopril.

M   Perfect, thank you that's very helpful. And have you had them this morning?

F	Yes, that's what the nurse told me at the pre-assessment, yes, so is that all right? Just with some water. I usually have them before breakfast but she said no food at all this morning.
M	Excellent. And apart from the high blood pressure do you have any other medical problems at all?
F	Err… Yes, I take some blood-thinning drugs because I had a small heart attack a bit ago, so I'm taking aspirin and… at the pre-assessment they said to keep on with them, so I had one this morning like I usually do. They told me to stop the other one … err, I can't remember the name …
M	Ahh… Warfarin?
F	No, it begins with c… err… clop…clopidogrel. Err... they told me to stop it a week before the operation. Seven days.
M	Fantastic
F	So I stopped last Tuesday.
M	Great. Now, tell me a bit more about this heart attack. How long ago was that?
F	Err… two years ago. My GP picked up on it.
M	Did that all go …
F	Yes, err… pretty good
M	And why did you go to your GP, were you having chest pains?
F	Err… they weren't chest pains, they were … I was just getting a bit breathless and it was difficult for me to tell what was going on but, err…Dr Scott picked up on it when I went to see him and he sent me to the cardiology team.
M	Right. Did they say you'd had a heart attack?
F	Yes, they told me I'd had a small one and so I had some stents put in … a couple of them.
M	And since they were done…
F	Yes, I've been better you know, I… err I don't feel so tired all the time
M	OK. And what can you do in terms of exercising?
F	Well I can do anything … anything really.
M	Mmm and, tell me what you can do.
F	Well we have stairs at home and we don't have a loo on the ground floor, it's on the first floor, so I'm up and down a few times a day.
M	And walking on the flat's fine?
F	Yes, that's OK.
M	Any problems with your ankles swelling?
F	Well this one it swells up if I've been standing. Alright, I had my veins done, my varicose veins. But, err the other one's alright. I sprained it quite badly last year but it's fine now.
M	Right. Erm, can I just ask you a few other questions about your heart.

F	Sure
M	Have you ever had any palpitations at all? When your heart goes boom boom boom.
F	No
M	You've never experienced any of those?
F	Well no… no. Not really. I mean if… if I run my heart beats a bit faster but that's normal isn't it.
M	Sure. Erm, anything else … any digestive problems?
F	No … well if I have a heavy meal late at night, like if… if I have pastry or something, I sometimes wake up in the night feeling a bit erm… like heartburn, erm… but if I take an anti-acid it's fine.
M	Right. So in general you sound to be in pretty good shape. Hmm now in a minute I'll tell you about exactly what type of anaesthesia we'll be using. But, first of all is there anything you'd like to ask me … do you have any concerns about anything?
F	Erm, well I suppose the main thing is after the operation, err, when I wake up… Erm I mean will I be in a lot of pain when I come round?
M	No, you'll be given morphine during the procedure and that will still be working when you wake up, and then when that wears off you'll be given something else. There'll be someone keeping an eye on you.
F	OK. Ohh… Err and the other thing is, Err I've heard that if you have crowns in your mouth they can get damaged if they put in an air tube.
M	Well, it's unlikely but we'll take special care. So which teeth are we talking about?
F	Err, these two.
M	OK the two central incisors. And do you have any other teeth with crowns or implants.
F	No.
M	OK. So what we have planned for you is …[fade]

PAUSE: 10 SECONDS
That is the end of Part A. Now, look at Part B.

PAUSE: 5 SECONDS
Part B. In this part of the test, you'll hear six different extracts. In each extract, you'll hear people talking in a different healthcare setting.

For questions 25 to 30, choose the answer A, B or C which fits best according to what you hear. You'll have time to read each question before you listen. Complete your answers as you listen.

Now look at Question 25. You hear two trainee doctors doing an activity at a staff training day. Now read the question.

PAUSE: 15 SECONDS
---***---

M	So what did the trainer say we have to do?

F   Well, we've got to look through these case notes – ten sets in total – and decide which of the patients should be referred to the consultant as a matter of urgency, and which can wait.

M   Oh right. And did I hear him say there's a limited number you can refer?

F   Not exactly. He said that we should put them in rank order according to the severity of the symptoms and other factors evident from the case notes. Once we've agreed on our list, we have to go and compare with another pair of trainees.

M   OK. Let's get started then.

PAUSE: 5 SECONDS
Question 26. You hear a radiographer talking to a patient about her MRI scan. Now read the question.

PAUSE: 15 SECONDS
---***---

M   Come in, come in. Mrs Brown, isn't it? My name's Ted and I'm going to be doing your MRI scan today. Now, can you get up on the table for me?

F   You know, I'm really claustrophobic.

M   Mm, well, this is a new piece of equipment. The diameter's much larger, so it should make it a little more comfortable for you. You'll also have this call bell, so if you need me at any point during the test you squeeze that, OK?

F   OK.

M   Now your scan's only going to take about 15 minutes. Are you OK with that?

F   I am.

M   OK. Let's get started then.

PAUSE: 5 SECONDS

Question 27. You hear two nurses discussing an article in a nursing journal. Now read the question.

PAUSE: 15 SECONDS
---***---

F: Did you see the article about research on strokes and sight problems in the latest Nursing magazine?

M: Yes, I found it interesting that there's quite such a high degree of visual impairment after a stroke.

F: Yeah, but I think I could've told them that without an expensive research study.

M: Well, you need evidence to get progress in how people are treated. And now there'll be a push for all stroke patients to have eye assessments as a matter of course.

F: It certainly makes a pretty solid case for that. Especially as there's plenty that can be done to help people if early screening diagnoses an issue.

M: Absolutely.

F: I was just sorry the article didn't provide more detail about the type of sight problems that are most common after a stroke.

M: Well there's a reference to where the whole study's been published - so you could always find out there.

PAUSE: 5 SECONDS

Question 28. You hear two hospital managers talking about a time management course for staff. Now read the question.

PAUSE: 15 SECONDS

---***---

M   The uptake for the course in time management for staff has been disappointing, hasn't it?

F   It has – but I'm not exactly sure why, because everyone seems to know about it. And we asked for it to be changed from a four-hour session to two two-hour slots to make it easier for nurses to be released from their wards. But apparently that wasn't possible because it has to be done a certain way.

M   Yeah, I'm not convinced that was the problem anyway. I think once staff become aware of what it's aiming to do, and how it fits together with other initiatives, there might be more interest.

F   Yeah. There certainly is a need, even if the staff themselves don't actually realise it at present.

PAUSE: 5 SECONDS
Question 29. You hear an optometrist reporting on some research he's been doing. Now read the question.

PAUSE: 15 SECONDS

---***---

M: I specialise in dealing with fungal eye infections. At present, treatment involves giving eye drops every hour for at least two weeks. I wanted to improve this process, by designing a system capable of releasing anti-fungal drugs onto the eye over an extended period. Contact lenses are perfect for this, as their hydrogel structure has the ability to uptake and release drugs, and their placement on the eye ensures the drug gets released directly to the cornea. In order to make a contact lens provide drugs over a sustained period, I've modified the lens. I've also used nanoparticles for packaging the drugs. So, I've managed to create a system capable of delivering an anti-fungal drug called Nanomycin for up to four hours. I now hope to increase this, and use this system with other drugs.

PAUSE: 5 SECONDS
Question 30. You hear a consultant talking to a trainee about a patient's eye condition. Now read the question.

PAUSE: 15 SECONDS

---***---

M	Have we got Mrs Kent's notes?
F	Yes, they're here. She's coming in today for possible laser surgery for her retinopathy, isn't she?
M	Well, depending on results – and from the look of these pictures we took last time, there's been a slow improvement, so we'll talk to her and perhaps hold off for the time being – unless her condition's worsened, 'cos it can in some cases.
F	So what's the cause?
M	Well, we know a leak of fluid behind the retina causes the distorted vision which sufferers get, but not why that occurs. There may be a link with stress, and also steroid use, but the jury's still out, I'm afraid.

PAUSE: 10 SECONDS
That is the end of Part B. Now, look at Part C.

PAUSE: 5 SECONDS
Part C. In this part of the test, you'll hear two different extracts. In each extract, you'll hear health professionals talking about aspects of their work.

For questions 31 to 42, choose the answer A, B or C which fits best according to what you hear. Complete your answers as you listen.

Now look at extract one.

Extract one. Questions 31 to 36. You hear an interview with a neurosurgeon called Dr Ian Marsh who specialises in the treatment of concussion in sport.

You now have 90 seconds to read questions 31 to 36.

PAUSE: 90 SECONDS
---***---

F:	My guest today is Dr Ian Marsh, a specialist in the treatment of concussion in sport and a co-author on a new set of guidelines. So, Dr Marsh, what's the aim of these new guidelines?
M:	Well the aim was really to provide a resource, not for the top-level professional sports people, but for parents, teachers and coaches of young people playing sport. The guidelines basically offer some expert information from a GP, an emergency physician, and myself as a neurosurgeon, about what the condition is, also how to identify the symptoms and how to manage it. If any of your listeners have ever had a concussion doing sports, you'll know how frightening it can be. It's confusing and painful, and difficult sometimes for teachers, parents, or whoever to work out if someone with concussion is okay. I mean… we hope to remedy that.
F:	And how do we know when someone is suffering from concussion?
M:	Well, obviously, if the person's actually knocked out – it's clear. But not all patients actually lose consciousness. Often following a hard knock to the head, they become disorientated or experience headaches, nausea or vomiting. These are signs of concussion and they may clear initially, but then return when the individual actually undertakes further physical activity; right, when they start to train, say. So, it can actually take quite a while for things to really clear up. The essence of it is that people shouldn't start playing again until those warning signs have completely subsided.

F: Yes, and you say that waiting anything less than fourteen days after all the symptoms have cleared would be too early to return?

M: Yeah, that's right. If they go back too early, they risk a second concussion and, as we know from professional athletes, they may have to give up their sport if they have too many concussions. Right, so it's better, particularly in a young person with a developing brain, to allow all of the symptoms to settle, and only then return to play — well usually return to train first, then return to play after that. It used to be thought that receiving another concussion, could lead to severe brain swelling, and that could be fatal or at least involve a visit to the emergency room. I think the evidence is fairly slim for that. What we do know though is that the compounding effect of having one concussion followed by another seems to be more severe than just the one. So it's always better to let the brain recover fully before playing again.

F: Right, so who's at the highest risk of sports concussion?

M: Well, actually a concussion can happen whenever anyone receives a blow to the head. Usually it's a sort of twisting blow, not a straight-on blow. But, obviously people playing sports like rugby - where there's bodily contact – stand more chance of being at the receiving end of such a blow. But having said that, it's just as likely to affect kids kicking a ball around a park as it is to affect top professional players in big matches.

F: Do you think that youth sports need specialist concussion doctors on hand? Like the professionals do?

M: There's always a risk and we know that it happens from time to time, but I mean most games — even the most dangerous ones — are without incident at all. I think people who are involved in running youth sports, whether they be referees, coaches, or parents, can be made aware of how to manage concussion, the signs that they need to look out for, and maybe the warnings of something more serious, so that they can take the appropriate actions. But I think always having a doctor on the sidelines where young people are playing is just an over-reaction.

F: In the USA, college football is big business. They're trialling helmet sensors and impact sensors. Do you think that's something we need everywhere?

M: Well, I don't think it'll come to that. I think there are two scenarios here. The first is one where a concussion's a one-off event following a significant blow to the head. Right, the second's quite different and involves Chronic Traumatic Encephalopathy. This comes about particularly in American Football, where players use their helmets and heads almost like weapons. That type of repeated impact seems to add up over the player's career. That's something we've heard being discussed, mostly in the USA. Naturally there's interest generally in protecting players, particularly in the professional levels of sport, but I see that as a different matter to the management of concussion itself.

PAUSE: 10 SECONDS
Now look at extract two.

Extract two. Questions 37 to 42. You hear a presentation by a consultant cardiologist called Dr Pamela Skelton, who's talking about a research trial called SPRINT which investigated the effects of setting lower blood-pressure targets.

You now have 90 seconds to read questions 37 to 42.

PAUSE: 90 SECONDS
---***---

F: Hello - I'm Dr Pamela Skelton, Consultant Cardiologist at this hospital, and I'm talking about the recent SPRINT study into the effects of setting lower blood-pressure targets, which in turn affects the advice and medication which patients are given. I'm going to describe the patients who were selected, how the trial was conducted and the implications of its results for us all as health professionals.

First – the trial itself. It involved over nine-thousand hypertensive participants, aged fifty-plus, most of whom were on blood-pressure medication. They were randomly assigned to one of two groups – one with a goal of less than one-hundred-and-twenty millimetres systolic BP, the other with a goal of less than one-hundred-and-forty millimetres, the traditional standard. The intention was to follow these patients for five years, factoring in the usual drop-out rate. As it turned out, however, the trial was stopped after just three years thanks to an all-cause mortality reduction of nearly thirty percent for the one-hundred-and-twenty group, which was definitive and shocking - but wonderful. As I mentioned, the participants were over-fifties and it goes without saying that as people age, they develop more diseases and health problems as a matter of course. But there was a specific group of over-seventy-fives who did just as well as younger patients.

Before the trial, some medics referred to the natural stiffening of the arteries with ageing, suggesting that a hundred-and-twenty was too low a target for the over-seventy-fives, risking an increase of dizzy spells which would affect general wellbeing. But this concern turned out to be unfounded. Others thought there'd be a failure to take the number of tablets needed to reach a BP of a hundred-and-twenty, especially among older participants. Again, this wasn't an issue - the average needed was just three per day. The over-seventy-fives, already on various drugs, didn't object to extra medication. Participants from this age group who didn't finish the trial were taken out because some conditions, which were already present, worsened; for example in some cases obesity levels rose too high.

To manage their blood pressure, participants were given standard drugs – nothing experimental, just drugs that are readily available and low-cost. Another key factor was that blood pressure was measured in a very specific way. Rather than give patients an arm cuff for at-home twenty-four-hour ambulatory monitoring, an automated machine was used at the hospital. This took three separate readings and averaged them. Also, readings were taken while staff were out of the room to avoid what's called 'white coat syndrome' in patients.

Now, some of you may be familiar with the ACCORD study into blood pressure levels several years ago, which in some respects was similar to SPRINT. There are some differences, though. For example, ACCORD was about half the size of SPRINT, and unlike SPRINT, the ACCORD study allowed diabetic patients to take part. Despite this, in general, the ACCORD participants were rather lower risk than those in the SPRINT trial – probably because of the slightly lower average age. The ACCORD trial didn't show a statistically significant benefit for overall cardiovascular outcomes, but there was a clear forty percent reduction in strokes – even though that was a secondary outcome.

So, to summarise, the SPRINT trial seems to support a hundred-and-twenty as a recommended blood-pressure target. This is doubtless a landmark study and, importantly, one which was sponsored by government rather than by the interests of the pharmaceutical corporations. I recommend a note of caution though, as SPRINT does contradict previous findings. The Cochrane View in 2011, for example, said that lowering to under a hundred and forty didn't produce a change in the risk of death overall. However, we must bear in mind that Cochrane was looking retrospectively at trials which weren't actually focused on the same particular issue. So it's worth doing a full and systematic evaluation, to see where the SPRINT trial fits in with what we already know.

It's interesting that a few GPs have already been working with older patients to hit lower blood-pressure goals, and the new data will doubtless encourage greater take-up of this more interventionist line of attack. But the SPRINT results don't mean that everyone with hypertension should be dropping to under a hundred-and-twenty. Plus, to achieve those lower levels, it's unlikely that lifestyle changes alone would be enough, it could well require several anti-hypertensive drugs as well. There remain some unanswered questions, of course - for example whether other groups, like those with a lower heart-attack risk, need to keep their blood pressure that low. So, while SPRINT can help guide doctors' decisions about some patients, it doesn't mean that a new universal standard for blood pressure is in order. Instead, it's a good reason for everyone to discuss with their doctor, their own ideal and particular target.

PAUSE: 10 SECONDS
That is the end of Part C.

You now have two minutes to check your answers.

PAUSE: 120 SECONDS
That is the end of the Listening test.

Reading sub-test
Answer Key – Part A

READING SUB-TEST – ANSWER KEY

PART A: QUESTIONS 1-20

1	B
2	A
3	C
4	A
5	D
6	A
7	organic matter
8	foreign bodies
9	compound
10	6/six hours
11	systemic sepsis
12	immuno(-)suppressed
13	antibiotics
14	(in) (the) jaw
15	broken bones
16	(a) bite reflex
17	5/five (times)
18	(a) booster dose OR booster doses
19	twenty-three/23 gauge
20	crying

Reading sub-test
Answer Key – Parts B & C

READING SUB-TEST – ANSWER KEY

PART B: QUESTIONS 1-6

1	B	there is severe leakage from the wound.
2	A	encourage participation in the scheme.
3	A	data about patient errors may be incomplete.
4	B	There are several ways of ensuring that the ventilator is working effectively.
5	C	the patients most likely to suffer complications.
6	B	to draw conclusions from the results of cleaning audits

PART C: QUESTIONS 7-14

7	C	lacks any form of convincing proof of its value as a treatment.
8	A	surprise at people's willingness to put their trust in it.
9	B	the key attraction of the approach for patients.
10	B	frequently result from a patient's treatment preferences.
11	C	the way that homeopathic remedies endanger more than just the user
12	D	the way positive results can be achieved despite people's doubts.
13	A	prepared to accept that homeopathy may depend on psychological factors.
14	D	the motivation behind the desire for homeopathy to gain scientific acceptance

PART C: QUESTIONS 15-22

15	A	It required intense concentration.
16	D	the connections between sensors and the brain need to be exact.
17	A	There was statistical evidence that it was successful.
18	B	Patients might have to undergo too many operations.
19	D	It is difficult for scientists to pinpoint precise areas with an electrode.
20	C	It may have more potential than electrical stimulation.
21	A	how much more there is to achieve.
22	B	to illustrate the fact that some sensation is better than none

OCCUPATIONAL ENGLISH TEST

WRITING SUB-TEST: MEDICINE

SAMPLE RESPONSE: LETTER OF REFERRAL

Dr Leigh Waters
Surgeon
Stillwater Private Hospital
54 Main Street
Stillwater

24. 02.2018

Dear Dr Waters,

Re: Mrs Carol Potter
DOB: 30.12.1947

Thank you for seeing Mrs Potter, 70 years old, for management of her left knee.

Mrs Potter has had bilateral osteoarthritis of her hands and knees for ten years. Over the last 12 months, Mrs Potter has experienced increased difficulty walking due to pain in her left knee. The pain even occurs while resting after a long walk, despite taking regular Panadol Osteo. There has been no joint swelling or recent injury.

On examination, she has a limited range of movement of her left knee due to pain but there is still no swelling. A recent X-ray of her left knee confirms severe osteoarthritis with osteophytes and loss of joint space. I believe this is the reason for her worsening symptoms.

Mrs Potter is normally well. She has well-controlled hypertension and has had urinary tract infections intermittently in the past. Recent blood tests (FBE and UEC) are normal. Mrs Potter's current medications include ramipril 5mg daily, Panadol Osteo 2 tablets t.d.s. and temazepam 10mg nocte as required. I have prescribed extra analgesia (naproxen 250 mg b.d.) and arranged for Mrs Potter to receive physiotherapy.

I would be grateful for your opinion as to whether a left knee joint replacement would be of benefit for Mrs Potter.

Yours sincerely,

Doctor

MEDICINE

PRACTICE TEST 3

To listen to the audio, visit
https://www.occupationalenglishtest.org/audio

LISTENING SUB-TEST – QUESTION PAPER

CANDIDATE NUMBER:

LAST NAME:

FIRST NAME:

MIDDLE NAMES:

PROFESSION:

VENUE:

TEST DATE:

Candidate details and photo will be printed here.

Passport Photo

CANDIDATE DECLARATION

By signing this, you agree not to disclose or use in any way (other than to take the test) or assist any other person to disclose or use any OET test or sub-test content. If you cheat or assist in any cheating, use any unfair practice, break any of the rules or regulations, or ignore any advice or information, you may be disqualified and your results may not be issued at the sole discretion of CBLA. CBLA also reserves its right to take further disciplinary action against you and to pursue any other remedies permitted by law. If a candidate is suspected of and investigated for malpractice, their personal details and details of the investigation may be passed to a third party where required.

CANDIDATE SIGNATURE: _____

TIME: APPROXIMATELY **40 MINUTES**

INSTRUCTIONS TO CANDIDATES

DO NOT open this question paper until you are told to do so.

One mark will be granted for each correct answer.

Answer **ALL** questions. Marks are **NOT** deducted for incorrect answers.

At the end of the test, you will have two minutes to check your answers.

At the end of the test, hand in this **Question Paper.**

You must not remove OET material from the test room.

HOW TO ANSWER THE QUESTIONS

Part A: Write your answers on this **Question Paper** by filling in the blanks. **Example: Patient:** _Ray Sands_

Part B & Part C: Mark your answers on this **Question Paper** by filling in the circle using a 2B pencil. **Example:** Ⓐ ● Ⓒ

www.occupationalenglishtest.org
© Cambridge Boxhill Language Assessment – ABN 51 988 559 414
[CANDIDATE NO.] LISTENING QUESTION PAPER 01/12

Occupational English Test
Listening Test

This test has three parts. In each part you'll hear a number of different extracts. At the start of each extract, you'll hear this sound: --beep—

You'll have time to read the questions before you hear each extract and you'll hear each extract **ONCE ONLY**. Complete your answers as you listen.

At the end of the test you'll have two minutes to check your answers.

Part A

In this part of the test, you'll hear two different extracts. In each extract, a health professional is talking to a patient.

For **questions 1-24**, complete the notes with information you hear.

Now, look at the notes for extract one.

Extract 1: Questions 1-12

You hear a pulmonologist talking to a patient called Robert Miller. For **questions 1-12**, complete the notes with a word or short phrase.

You now have 30 seconds to look at the notes.

Patient	Robert Miller
Symptoms	• tiredness
	• persistent **(1)** _____ cough
	• SOB
	• weight loss described as **(2)** _____ in nature.
	• fingertips appear **(3)** _____
	• nails feel relatively **(4)** _____
Background details	• previously employed as a **(5)** _____ (20 yrs)
	• now employed as a **(6)** _____
	• no longer able to play golf
	• keeps pigeons as a hobby
Medical history	• last year diagnosed with hypertension
	• current prescription of **(7)** _____
	• **(8)** _____ sounds in chest reported by GP
	• father suffered from **(9)** _____
Previous tests	• **(10)** _____ six months ago
	• chest x-ray one month ago
Future actions	• **(11)** _____ test
	• CT scan
	• prescription of **(12)** _____ (possibly)

Extract 2: Questions 13-24

You hear an eye specialist talking to a patient called Jasmine Burton, who has recently undergone eye surgery. For **questions 13-24**, complete the notes with a word or short phrase.

You now have thirty seconds to look at the notes.

Patient   Jasmine Burton

Patient history
- suffers from **(13)** _____ astigmatism
- also has **(14)** _____ (so surgery under general anaesthetic)
- eye problems may result from a lack of **(15)** _____
- sight problems mean **(16)** _____ isn't an option for her
- reports some slowness to **(17)** _____
- has poor perception of **(18)** _____
- works as a **(19)** _____
  - reports having no issues at work
- eyes checked every few years

Surgery
- **(20)** _____ in right eye first noted three years ago
- February this year - had surgery
- some capsular **(21)** _____ noted post-operatively
- examination showed no sign of a **(22)** _____
  - follow up appointment in 6 months

Presenting with
- reported increase in number of **(23)** _____
- increased sensitivity to **(24)** _____

That is the end of Part A. Now look at Part B.

146   PRACTICE TEST **3**

Part B

In this part of the test, you'll hear six different extracts. In each extract, you'll hear people talking in a different healthcare setting.

For **questions 25-30**, choose the answer (**A**, **B** or **C**) which fits best according to what you hear. You'll have time to read each question before you listen. Complete your answers as you listen.

Now look at question 25.

25. You hear a nurse briefing a colleague at the end of her shift.

    What does the colleague have to do for the patient tonight?

    A   remove her saline drip

    B   arrange for more tests

    C   monitor her blood pressure

26. You hear part of a hospital management meeting where a concern is being discussed.

    What is the committee concerned about?

    A   poor response to recruitment drives

    B   difficulties in retaining suitable staff

    C   relatively high staff absence rates

27. You hear a GP and his practice nurse discussing a vaccination programme.

    They agree that the practice should

    A   make sure patients are aware of it.

    B   organise it more effectively than in the past.

    C   prepare to cope with an increasing demand for it.

28. You hear two hospital nurses discussing the assessment of a patient on their ward.

What is the problem?

- (A) The patient's documentation has been sent to the wrong place.
- (B) Nobody has taken responsibility for assessing the patient.
- (C) The duty doctor was unable to locate the patient.

29. You hear the beginning of a training session for dental students.

The trainer is explaining that the session will

- (A) focus on aspects of dental hygiene.
- (B) expand upon what they studied previously.
- (C) introduce them to a completely new technique.

30. You hear two nurses discussing the treatment of a patient with a kidney infection.

What is the female nurse doing?

- (A) emphasising the urgency of a procedure
- (B) suggesting how to overcome a difficulty
- (C) warning him about a possible problem

That is the end of Part B. Now look at Part C.

Part C

In this part of the test, you'll hear two different extracts. In each extract, you'll hear health professionals talking about aspects of their work.

For **questions 31-42**, choose the answer (**A, B** or **C**) which fits best according to what you hear. Complete your answers as you listen.

Now look at extract one.

Extract 1: Questions 31-36

You hear a geriatrician called Dr Clare Cox giving a presentation on the subject of end-of-life care for people with dementia.

You now have 90 seconds to read **questions 31-36**.

31. What problem does Dr Cox identify concerning dementia patients?

    A   They can often make unrealistic demands on their carers.

    B   Their condition can develop in a number of different ways.

    C   The type of care that they may require is extremely costly.

32. Why did *Dementia Australia* decide to examine the issue of end-of-life dementia care?

    A   There was a lack of reliable information on it.

    B   The number of stories about poor care made it urgent.

    C   There were enough data on which to base an effective care plan.

33. For Dr Cox, the initial results of the dementia survey reveal that palliative care

    A   was working more effectively than people had thought.

    B   was more widely available than some users imagined.

    C   was viewed negatively by medical professionals.

PRACTICE TEST **3**   149

34. Dr Cox says that lack of knowledge of the law by care professionals

- A proves that family members should help make pain management decisions.
- B could be resulting in a surprisingly high number of premature deaths.
- C may lead to dementia patients experiencing unnecessary distress.

35. Dr Cox thinks that the statistics she quotes on refusing treatment

- A illustrate a gap in current medical education programmes.
- B show how patients' wishes are too often misunderstood by carers.
- C demonstrate the particular difficulties presented by dementia patients.

36. Dr Cox makes the point that end-of-life planning is desirable because

- A it reduces the complexity of certain care decisions.
- B it avoids carers having to speculate about a patient's wishes.
- C it ensures that everyone receives the best possible quality of care.

Now look at extract two.

Extract 2: Questions 37-42

You hear a hospital doctor called Dr Keith Gardiner giving a presentation about some research he's done on the subject of staff-patient communication.

You now have 90 seconds to read **questions 37-42**.

37. Dr Gardiner first became interested in staff-patient communication after

    (A) experiencing poor communication as an in-patient.

    (B) observing the effects of poor communication on a patient.

    (C) analysing patient feedback data on the subject of communication.

38. What point does Dr Gardiner make about a typical admission to hospital?

    (A) The information given can overwhelm patients.

    (B) Patients often feel unable to communicate effectively.

    (C) Filling in detailed paperwork can be stressful for patients.

39. Dr Gardiner uses an example of poor communication to illustrate the point that

    (A) patients should be consulted about the desirability of a hospital stay.

    (B) specialists need to be informed if there are any mental health issues.

    (C) relatives' knowledge of a patient's condition shouldn't be taken for granted.

40. Dr Gardiner explains that a survey conducted among in-patients about communication

- (A) measured the difference between their expectations and their actual experience.
- (B) asked their opinion about all aspects of the service they received.
- (C) included questions on how frequently they visited the hospital.

41. One common complaint arising from Dr Gardner's survey concerned

- (A) a lack of privacy for patients receiving sensitive information.
- (B) the over-use of unclear medical terminology with patients.
- (C) a tendency not to address patients in a respectful way.

42. How does Dr Gardiner feel about the results of the survey?

- (A) surprised by one response from patients
- (B) reassured by the level of patient care identified
- (C) worried that unforeseen problems were highlighted

That is the end of Part C.

You now have two minutes to check your answers.

END OF THE LISTENING TEST

READING SUB-TEST – TEXT BOOKLET: PART A

CANDIDATE NUMBER:

LAST NAME:

FIRST NAME:

MIDDLE NAMES:

PROFESSION:

VENUE:

TEST DATE:

Candidate details and photo will be printed here.

Passport Photo

CANDIDATE DECLARATION

By signing this, you agree not to disclose or use in any way (other than to take the test) or assist any other person to disclose or use any OET test or sub-test content. If you cheat or assist in any cheating, use any unfair practice, break any of the rules or regulations, or ignore any advice or information, you may be disqualified and your results may not be issued at the sole discretion of CBLA. CBLA also reserves its right to take further disciplinary action against you and to pursue any other remedies permitted by law. If a candidate is suspected of and investigated for malpractice, their personal details and details of the investigation may be passed to a third party where required.

CANDIDATE SIGNATURE: _____

INSTRUCTIONS TO CANDIDATES

You must **NOT** remove OET material from the test room.

www.occupationalenglishtest.org
© Cambridge Boxhill Language Assessment – ABN 51 988 559 414

[CANDIDATE NO.] READING TEXT BOOKLET PART A 01/04

Necrotizing Fasciitis (NF): Texts

Text A

Necrotizing fasciitis (NF) is a severe, rare, potentially lethal soft tissue infection that develops in the scrotum and perineum, the abdominal wall, or the extremities. The infection progresses rapidly, and septic shock may ensue; hence, the mortality rate is high (median mortality 32.2%). NF is classified into four types, depending on microbiological findings.

Table 1

Classification of responsible pathogens according to type of infection

Microbiological type	Pathogens	Site of infection	Co-morbidities
Type 1 (polymicrobial)	Obligate and facultative anaerobes	Trunk and perineum	Diabetes mellitus
Type 2 (monomicrobial)	Beta-hemolytic streptococcus A	Limbs	
Type 3	Clostridium species Gram-negative bacteria Vibrios spp. Aeromonas hydrophila	Limbs, trunk and perineum	Trauma Seafood consumption (for Aeromonas)
Type 4	Candida spp. Zygomycetes	Limbs, trunk, perineum	Immuno-suppression

Text B

Antibiotic treatment for NF

Type 1
- Initial treatment includes ampicillin or ampicillin–sulbactam combined with metronidazole or clindamycin.
- Broad gram-negative coverage is necessary as an initial empirical therapy for patients who have recently been treated with antibiotics, or been hospitalized. In such cases, antibiotics such as ampicillin–sulbactam, piperacillin–tazobactam, ticarcillin–clavulanate acid, third or fourth generation cephalosporins, or carbapenems are used, and at a higher dosage.

Type 2
- First or second generation of cephalosporins are used for the coverage of methicillin-sensitive Staphylococcus aureus (MSSA).
- MRSA tends to be covered by vancomycin, or daptomycin and linezolid in cases where S. aureus is resistant to vancomycin.

Type 3
- NF should be managed with clindamycin and penicillin, which kill the Clostridium species.
- If Vibrio infection is suspected, the early use of tetracyclines (including doxycycline and minocycline) and third-generation cephalosporins is crucial for the survival of the patient, since these antibiotics have been shown to reduce the mortality rate drastically.

Type 4
- Can be treated with amphotericin B or fluoroconazoles, but the results of this treatment are generally disappointing.

Antibiotics should be administered for up to 5 days after local signs and symptoms have resolved. The mean duration of antibiotic therapy for NF is 4–6 weeks.

Text C

Supportive care in an ICU is critical to NF survival. This involves fluid resuscitation, cardiac monitoring, aggressive wound care, and adequate nutritional support. Patients with NF are in a catabolic state and require increased caloric intake to combat infection. This can be delivered orally or via nasogastric tube, peg tube, or intravenous hyperalimentation. This should begin immediately (within the first 24 hours of hospitalization). Prompt and aggressive support has been shown to lower complication rates. Baseline and repeated monitoring of albumin, prealbumin, transferrin, blood urea nitrogen, and triglycerides should be performed to ensure the patient is receiving adequate nutrition.

Wound care is also an important concern. Advanced wound dressings have replaced wet-to-dry dressings. These dressings promote granulation tissue formation and speed healing. Advanced wound dressings may lend to healing or prepare the wound bed for grafting. A healthy wound bed increases the chances of split-thickness skin graft take. Vacuum-assisted closure (VAC) was recently reported to be effective in a patient whose cardiac status was too precarious to undergo a long surgical reconstruction operation. With the VAC., the patient's wound decreased in size, and the VAC was thought to aid in local management of infection and improve granulation tissue.

Text D

Advice to give the patient before discharge

- Help arrange the patient's aftercare, including home health care and instruction regarding wound management, social services to promote adjustment to lifestyle changes and financial concerns, and physical therapy sessions to help rebuild strength and promote the return to optimal physical health.
- The life-threatening nature of NF, scarring caused by the disease, and in some cases the need for limb amputation can alter the patient's attitude and viewpoint, so be sure to take a holistic approach when dealing with the patient and family.

Remind the diabetic patient to

- control blood glucose levels, keeping the glycated haemoglobin (HbAlc) level to 7% or less.
- keep needles capped until use and not to reuse needles.
- clean the skin thoroughly before blood glucose testing or insulin injection, and to use alcohol pads to clean the area afterward.

END OF PART A

THIS TEXT BOOKLET WILL BE COLLECTED

READING SUB-TEST – QUESTION PAPER: PART A

CANDIDATE NUMBER:

LAST NAME:

FIRST NAME:

MIDDLE NAMES:

PROFESSION:

VENUE:

TEST DATE:

Candidate details and photo will be printed here.

Passport Photo

CANDIDATE DECLARATION

By signing this, you agree not to disclose or use in any way (other than to take the test) or assist any other person to disclose or use any OET test or sub-test content. If you cheat or assist in any cheating, use any unfair practice, break any of the rules or regulations, or ignore any advice or information, you may be disqualified and your results may not be issued at the sole discretion of CBLA. CBLA also reserves its right to take further disciplinary action against you and to pursue any other remedies permitted by law. If a candidate is suspected of and investigated for malpractice, their personal details and details of the investigation may be passed to a third party where required.

CANDIDATE SIGNATURE: _____

TIME: 15 MINUTES

INSTRUCTIONS TO CANDIDATES

DO NOT open this **Question Paper** or the **Text Booklet** until you are told to do so.

Write your answers on the spaces provided on this **Question Paper.**

You must answer the questions within the 15-minute time limit.

One mark will be granted for each correct answer.

Answer **ALL** questions. Marks are **NOT** deducted for incorrect answers.

At the end of the 15 minutes, hand in this **Question Paper** and the **Text Booklet.**

DO NOT remove OET material from the test room.

www.occupationalenglishtest.org
© Cambridge Boxhill Language Assessment – ABN 51 988 559 414

[CANDIDATE NO.] READING QUESTION PAPER PART A 01/04

Part A

TIME: 15 minutes

- Look at the four texts, **A-D**, in the separate **Text Booklet**.
- For each question, **1-20**, look through the texts, **A-D**, to find the relevant information.
- Write your answers on the spaces provided in this **Question Paper**.
- Answer all the questions within the 15-minute time limit.
- Your answers should be correctly spelt.

Necrotizing Fasciitis (NF): Questions

Questions 1-7

For each question, **1-7**, decide which text (**A**, **B**, **C** or **D**) the information comes from. You may use any letter more than once.

In which text can you find information about

1	the drug treatment required?	_____
2	which parts of the body can be affected?	_____
3	the various ways calories can be introduced?	_____
4	who to contact to help the patient after they leave hospital?	_____
5	what kind of dressing to use?	_____
6	how long to give drug therapy to the patient?	_____
7	what advice to give the patient regarding needle use?	_____

Questions 8-14

Answer each of the questions, **8-14**, with a word or short phrase from one of the texts. Each answer may include words, numbers or both.

8 Which two drugs can you use to treat the clostridium species of pathogen?

_____

9 Which common metabolic condition may occur with NF?

_____

10 What complication can a patient suffer from if NF isn't treated quickly enough?

_____

11 What procedure can you use with a wound if the patient can't be operated on?

_____

12   What should the patient be told to use to clean an injection site?

   _____

13   Which two drugs can be used if you can't use vancomycin?

   _____

14   What kind of infection should you use tetracyclines for?

   _____

Questions 15-20

Complete each of the sentences, **15-20**, with a word or short phrase from one of the texts. Each answer may include words, numbers or both.

15   The average proportion of patients who die as a result of contracting NF is _____.

16   Patients who have eaten _____ may be infected with Aeromonas hydrophilia.

17   Patients with Type 2 infection usually present with infected _____.

18   Type 1 NF is also known as _____.

19   The patient needs to be aware of the need to keep glycated haemoglobin levels lower than _____.

20   The patient will need a course of _____ to regain fitness levels after returning home.

END OF PART A
THIS QUESTION PAPER WILL BE COLLECTED

READING SUB-TEST – QUESTION PAPER: PARTS B & C

CANDIDATE NUMBER:

LAST NAME:

FIRST NAME:

MIDDLE NAMES:

PROFESSION:

VENUE:

TEST DATE:

Candidate details and photo will be printed here.

Passport Photo

CANDIDATE DECLARATION

By signing this, you agree not to disclose or use in any way (other than to take the test) or assist any other person to disclose or use any OET test or sub-test content. If you cheat or assist in any cheating, use any unfair practice, break any of the rules or regulations, or ignore any advice or information, you may be disqualified and your results may not be issued at the sole discretion of CBLA. CBLA also reserves its right to take further disciplinary action against you and to pursue any other remedies permitted by law. If a candidate is suspected of and investigated for malpractice, their personal details and details of the investigation may be passed to a third party where required.

CANDIDATE SIGNATURE: _____

TIME: 45 MINUTES

INSTRUCTIONS TO CANDIDATES

DO NOT open this **Question Paper** until you are told to do so.

One mark will be granted for each correct answer.

Answer **ALL** questions. Marks are **NOT** deducted for incorrect answers.

At the end of the test, hand in this **Question Paper**.

HOW TO ANSWER THE QUESTIONS:

Mark your answers on this **Question Paper** by filling in the circle using a 2B pencil. **Example:** Ⓐ Ⓑ Ⓒ

www.occupationalenglishtest.org
© Cambridge Boxhill Language Assessment – ABN 51 988 559 414
[CANDIDATE NO.] READING QUESTION PAPER PARTS B & C 01/16

Part B

In this part of the test, there are six short extracts relating to the work of health professionals. For **questions 1-6**, choose answer (**A**, **B** or **C**) which you think fits best according to the text.

1. The policy document tells us that

    A   stop dates aren't relevant in all circumstances.

    B   anyone using EPMA can disregard the request for a stop date.

    C   prescribers must know in advance of prescribing what the stop date should be.

Prescribing stop dates

Prescribers should write a review date or a stop date on the electronic prescribing system EPMA or the medicine chart for each antimicrobial agent prescribed. On the EPMA, there is a forced entry for stop dates on oral antimicrobials. There is not a forced stop date on EPMA for IV antimicrobial treatment – if the prescriber knows how long the course of IV should be, then the stop date can be filled in. If not known, then a review should be added to the additional information, e.g. 'review after 48 hrs'. If the prescriber decides treatment needs to continue beyond the stop date or course length indicated, then it is their responsibility to amend the chart. In critical care, it has been agreed that the routine use of review/stop dates on the charts is not always appropriate.

2. The guidelines inform us that personalised equipment for radiotherapy

- (A) is advisable for all patients.
- (B) improves precision during radiation.
- (C) needs to be tested at the first consultation.

Guidelines: Radiotherapy Simulation Planning Appointment

The initial appointment may also be referred to as the Simulation Appointment. During this appointment you will discuss your patient's medical history and treatment options, and agree on a radiotherapy treatment plan. The first step is usually to take a CT scan of the area requiring treatment. The patient will meet the radiation oncologist, their registrar and radiation therapists. A decision will be made regarding the best and most comfortable position for treatment, and this will be replicated daily for the duration of the treatment. Depending on the area of the body to be treated, personalised equipment such as a face mask may be used to stabilise the patient's position. This equipment helps keep the patient comfortable and still during the treatment and makes the treatment more accurate.

3. The purpose of these instructions is to explain how to

   (A) monitor an ECG reading.

   (B) position electrodes correctly.

   (C) handle an animal during an ECG procedure.

CT200CV Veterinarian Electrocardiograph User Manual

Animal connections

Good electrode connection is the most important factor in recording a high quality ECG. By following a few basic steps, consistent, clean recordings can be achieved.

1. Shave a patch on each forelimb of the animal at the contact site.

2. Clean the electrode sites with an alcohol swab or sterilising agent.

3. Attach clips to the ECG leads.

4. Place a small amount of ECG electrode gel on the metal electrode of the limb strap or adapter clip.

5. Pinch skin on animal and place clips on the shaved skin area of the animal being tested. The animal must be kept still.

6. Check the LCD display for a constant heart reading.

7. If there is no heart reading, you have a contact problem with one or more of the leads.

8. Recheck the leads and reapply the clips to the shaven skin of the animal.

4. The group known as 'impatient patients' are more likely to continue with a course of prescribed medication if

- (A) their treatment can be completed over a reduced period of time.

- (B) it is possible to link their treatment with a financial advantage.

- (C) its short-term benefits are explained to them.

Medication adherence and impatient patients

A recent article addressed the behaviour of people who have a 'taste for the present rather than the future'. It proposed that these so-called 'impatient patients' are unlikely to adhere to medications that require use over an extended period. The article proposes that, an 'impatience genotype' exists and that assessing these patients' view of the future while stressing the immediate advantages of adherence may improve adherence rates more than emphasizing potentially distant complications. The authors suggest that rather than attempting to change the character of those who are 'impatient', it may be wise to ascertain the patient's individual priorities, particularly as they relate to immediate gains. For example, while advising an 'impatient' patient with diabetes, stressing improvement in visual acuity rather than avoidance of retinopathy may result in greater medication adherence rates. Additionally, linking the cost of frequently changing prescription lenses when visual acuity fluctuates with glycemic levels may sometimes provide the patient with an immediate financial motivation for improving adherence.

5. The memo reminds nursing staff to avoid

   (A) x-raying a patient unless pH readings exceed 5.5.

   (B) the use of a particular method of testing pH levels.

   (C) reliance on pH testing in patients taking acid-inhibiting medication.

Checking the position of a nasogastric tube
It is essential to confirm the position of the tube in the stomach by one of the following: • Testing pH of aspirate: gastric placement is indicated by a pH of less than 4, but may increase to between pH 4-6 if the patient is receiving acid-inhibiting drugs. Blue litmus paper is insufficiently sensitive to adequately distinguish between levels of acidity of aspirate. • X-rays: will only confirm position at the time the X-ray is carried out. The tube may have moved by the time the patient has returned to the ward. In the absence of a positive aspirate test, where pH readings are more than 5.5, or in a patient who is unconscious or on a ventilator, an X-ray must be obtained to confirm the initial position of the nasogastric tube.

6. This extract informs us that

- **A** the amount of oxytocin given will depend on how the patient reacts.
- **B** the patient will go into labour as soon as oxytocin is administered.
- **C** the staff should inspect the oxytocin pump before use.

Extract from guidelines: Oxytocin

1 Oxytocin Dosage and Administration

Parenteral drug products should be inspected visually for particulate matter and discoloration prior to administration, whenever solution and container permit. Dosage of Oxytocin is determined by the uterine response. The dosage information below is based upon various regimens and indications in general use.

1.1 Induction or Stimulation of Labour

Intravenous infusion (drip method) is the only acceptable method of administration for the induction or stimulation of labour. Accurate control of the rate of infusion flow is essential. An infusion pump or other such device and frequent monitoring of strength of contractions and foetal heart rate are necessary for the safe administration of Oxytocin for the induction or stimulation of labour. If uterine contractions become too powerful, the infusion can be abruptly stopped, and oxytocic stimulation of the uterine musculature will soon wane.

Part C

In this part of the test, there are two texts about different aspects of healthcare. For **questions 7-22**, choose the answer (**A**, **B**, **C** or **D**) which you think fits best according to the text.

Text 1: Phobia pills

An irrational fear, or phobia, can cause the heart to pound and the pulse to race. It can lead to a full-blown panic attack – and yet the sufferer is not in any real peril. All it takes is a glimpse of, for example, a spider's web for the mind and body to race into panicked overdrive. These fears are difficult to conquer, largely because, although there are no treatment guidelines specifically about phobias, the traditional way of helping the sufferer is to expose them to the fear numerous times. Through the cumulative effect of these experiences, sufferers should eventually feel an increasing sense of control over their phobia. For some people, the process is too protracted, but there may be a short cut. Drugs that work to boost learning may help someone with a phobia to 'detrain' their brain, losing the fearful associations that fuel the panic.

The brain's extraordinary ability to store new memories and forge associations is so well celebrated that its **dark side** is often disregarded. A feeling of contentment is easily evoked when we see a photo of loved ones, though the memory may sometimes be more idealised than exact. In the case of a phobia, however, a nasty experience with, say, spiders, that once triggered a panicked reaction, leads the feelings to resurge whenever the relevant cue is seen again. The current approach is exposure therapy, which uses a process called extinction learning. This involves people being gradually exposed to whatever triggers their phobia until they feel at ease with it. As the individual becomes more comfortable with each situation, the brain automatically creates a new memory – one that links the cue with reduced feelings of anxiety, rather than the sensations that mark the onset of a panic attack.

Unfortunately, while it is relatively easy to create a fear-based memory, expunging that fear is more complicated. Each exposure trial will involve a certain degree of distress in the patient, and although the process is carefully managed throughout to limit this, some psychotherapists have concluded that the treatment is unethical. Neuroscientists have been looking for new ways to speed up extinction learning **for that same reason**.

One such avenue is the use of 'cognitive enhancers' such as a drug called D-cycloserine or DCS. DCS slots into part of the brain's 'NMDA receptor' and seems to modulate the neurons' ability to adjust their signalling in response to events. This tuning of a neuron's firing is thought to be one of the key ways the brain stores memories, and, at very low doses, DCS appears to boost that process, improving our ability to learn. In 2004, a team from Emory University in Atlanta, USA, tested whether DCS could also help people with phobias. A pilot trial was conducted on 28 people undergoing specific exposure therapy for acrophobia – a fear of heights. Results showed that those given a small amount of DCS alongside their regular therapy were able to reduce their phobia to a greater extent than those given a placebo. Since then, other groups have replicated the finding in further trials.

For people undergoing exposure therapy, achieving just one of the steps on the long journey to overcoming their fears requires considerable perseverance, says Cristian Sirbu, a behavioural scientist and psychologist. Thanks to improvement being so slow, patients – often already anxious – tend to feel they have failed. But Sirbu thinks that DCS may make it possible to tackle the problem in a single 3-hour session, which is enough for the patient to make real headway and to leave with a feeling of satisfaction. However, some people have misgivings about this approach, claiming that as it doesn't directly undo the fearful response which is deep-seated in the memory, there is a very real risk of relapse.

Rather than simply attempting to overlay the fearful associations with new ones, Merel Kindt at the University of Amsterdam is instead trying to alter the associations at source. Kindt's studies into anxiety disorders are based on the idea that memories are not only vulnerable to alteration when they're first laid down, but, of key importance, also at later retrieval. This allows for memories to be 'updated', and these amended memories are re-consolidated by the effect of proteins which alter synaptic responses, thereby maintaining the strength of feeling associated with the original memory. Kindt's team has produced encouraging results with arachnophobic patients by giving them propranolol, a well-known and well-tolerated beta-blocker drug, while they looked at spiders. This blocked the effects of norepinephrine in the brain, disrupting the way the memory was put back into storage after being retrieved, as part of the process of reconsolidation. Participants reported that while they still don't like spiders, they were able to approach them. Kindt reports that the benefit was still there three months after the test ended.

Text 1: Questions 7-14

7. In the first paragraph, the writer says that conventional management of phobias can be problematic because of

- (A) the lasting psychological effects of the treatment.
- (B) the time required to identify the cause of the phobia.
- (C) the limited choice of therapies available to professionals.
- (D) the need for the phobia to be confronted repeatedly over time.

8. In the second paragraph, the writer uses the phrase '**dark side**' to reinforce the idea that

- (A) memories of agreeable events tend to be inaccurate.
- (B) positive memories can be negatively distorted over time.
- (C) unhappy memories are often more detailed than happy ones.
- (D) unpleasant memories are aroused in response to certain prompts.

9. In the second paragraph, extinction learning is explained as a process which

- (A) makes use of an innate function of the brain.
- (B) encourages patients to analyse their particular fears.
- (C) shows patients how to react when having a panic attack.
- (D) focuses on a previously little-understood part of the brain.

10. What does the phrase '**for that same reason**' refer to?

- (A) the anxiety that patients feel during therapy
- (B) complaints from patients who feel unsupported
- (C) the conflicting ethical concerns of neuroscientists
- (D) psychotherapists who take on unsuitable patients

11. In the fourth paragraph, we learn that the drug called DCS

- (A) is unsafe to use except in small quantities.
- (B) helps to control only certain types of phobias.
- (C) affects how neurons in the brain react to stimuli.
- (D) increases the emotional impact of certain events.

12. In the fifth paragraph, some critics believe that one drawback of using DCS is that

- (A) its benefits are likely to be of limited duration.
- (B) it is only helpful for certain types of personality.
- (C) few patients are likely to complete the course of treatment.
- (D) patients feel discouraged by their apparent lack of progress.

13. In the final paragraph, we learn that Kindt's studies into anxiety disorders focused on how

- (A) proteins can affect memory retrieval.
- (B) memories are superimposed on each other.
- (C) negative memories can be reduced in frequency.
- (D) the emotional force of a memory is naturally retained.

14. The writer suggests that propranolol may

- (A) not offer a permanent solution for patients' phobias.
- (B) increase patients' tolerance of key triggers.
- (C) produce some beneficial side-effects.
- (D) be inappropriate for certain phobias.

Text 2: Challenging medical thinking on placebos

Dr Damien Finniss, Associate Professor at Sydney University's Pain Management and Research Institute, was previously a physiotherapist. He regularly treated football players during training sessions using therapeutic ultrasound. 'One particular session', Finniss explains, 'I treated five or six athletes. I'd treat them for five or ten minutes and they'd say, "I feel much better" and run back onto the field. But at the end of the session, I realised the ultrasound wasn't on.' It was a light bulb moment that set Finniss on the path to becoming a leading researcher on the placebo effect.

Used to treat depression, psoriasis and Parkinson's, to name but a few, placebos have an image problem among medics. For years, the thinking has been that a placebo is useless unless the doctor convinces the patient that it's a genuine treatment – problematic for a profession that promotes informed consent. However, a new study casts doubt on this assumption and, along with a swathe of research showing some remarkable results with placebos, raises questions about whether they should now enter the mainstream as legitimate prescription items. The study examined five trials in which participants were told they were getting a placebo, and the conclusion was that doing so honestly can work.

'If the evidence is there, I don't see the harm in openly administering a placebo,' says Ben Colagiuri, a researcher at the University of Sydney. Colagiuri recently published a meta-analysis of thirteen studies which concluded that placebo sleeping pills, whose genuine counterparts **notch up** nearly three million prescriptions in Australia annually, significantly improve sleep quality. The use of placebos could therefore reduce medical costs and the burden of disease in terms of adverse reactions.

But the placebo effect isn't just about fake treatments. It's about raising patients' expectations of a positive result; something which also occurs with real drugs. Finniss cites the 'open-hidden' effect, whereby an analgesic can be twice as effective if the patient knows they're getting it, compared to receiving it unknowingly. 'Treatment is always part medical and part ritual,' says Finniss. This includes the austere consulting room and even the doctor's clothing. But behind the performance of healing is some strong science. Simply believing an analgesic will work activates the same brain regions as the genuine drug. 'Part of the outcome of what we do is the way we interact with patients,' says Finniss.

That interaction is also the focus of Colagiuri's research. He's looking into the 'nocebo' effect, when a patient's pessimism about a treatment becomes self-fulfilling. 'If you give a placebo, and warn only 50% of the patients about side effects, those you warn report more side effects,' says Colagiuri. He's aiming to reverse that by exploiting the psychology of food packaging. Products are labelled '98% fat-free' rather than '2% fat' because positive reference to the word 'fat' puts consumers off. Colagiuri is deploying similar tactics. A drug with a 30% chance of causing a side effect can be reframed as having a 70% chance of not causing it. 'You're giving the same information, but framing it a way that minimises negative expectations,' says Colagiuri.

There is also a body of research showing that a placebo can produce a genuine biological response that could affect the disease process itself. It can be traced back to a study from the 1970s, when psychologist Robert Ader was trying to condition taste-aversion in rats. He gave them a saccharine drink whilst simultaneously injecting Cytoxan, an immune-suppressant which causes nausea. The rats learned to hate the drink due to the nausea. But as Ader continued giving it to them, without Cytoxan, they began to die from infection. Their immune system had 'learned' to fail by repeated pairing of the drink with Cytoxan. Professor Andrea Evers of Leiden University is running a study that capitalises on this conditioning effect and may benefit patients with rheumatoid arthritis, which causes the immune system to attack the joints. Evers' patients are given the immunosuppressant methotrexate, but instead of always receiving the same dose, they get a higher dose followed by a lower one. The theory is that the higher dose will cause the body to link the medication with a damped-down immune system. The lower dose will then work because the body has 'learned' to curb immunity as a placebo response to taking the drug. Evers hopes it will mean effective drug regimes that use lower doses with fewer side effects.

The medical profession, however, remains less than enthusiastic about placebos. 'I'm one of two researchers in the country who speak on placebos, and I've been invited to lecture at just one university,' says Finniss. According to Charlotte Blease, a philosopher of science, this antipathy may go to the core of what it means to be a doctor. 'Medical education is largely about biomedical facts. 'Softer' sciences, such as psychology, get marginalised because it's the hard stuff that's associated with what it means to be a doctor.' The result, says Blease, is a large, placebo-shaped hole in the medical curriculum. 'There's a great deal of medical illiteracy about the placebo effect ... it's the science behind the art of medicine. Doctors need training in that.'

Text 2: Questions 15-22

15. A football training session sparked Dr Finniss' interest in the placebo effect because

    A he saw for himself how it could work in practice.

    B he took the opportunity to try out a theory about it.

    C he made a discovery about how it works with groups.

    D he realised he was more interested in research than treatment.

16. The writer suggests that doctors should be more willing to prescribe placebos now because

    A research indicates that they are effective even without deceit.

    B recent studies are more reliable than those conducted in the past.

    C they have been accepted as a treatment by many in the profession.

    D they have been shown to relieve symptoms in a wide range of conditions.

17. What is suggested about sleeping pills by the use of the verb '**notch up**'?

    A they may have negative results

    B they could easily be replaced

    C they are extremely effective

    D they are very widely used

18. What point does the writer make in the fourth paragraph?

    A The way a treatment is presented is significant even if it is a placebo.

    B The method by which a drug is administered is more important than its content.

    C The theatrical side of medicine should not be allowed to detract from the science.

    D The outcome of a placebo treatment is affected by whether the doctor believes in it.

19. In researching side effects, Colagiuri aims to

    A   discover whether placebos can cause them.

    B   reduce the number of people who experience them.

    C   make information about them more accessible to patients.

    D   investigate whether pessimistic patients are more likely to suffer from them.

20. What does the word 'it' in the sixth paragraph refer to?

    A   a placebo treatment

    B   the disease process itself

    C   a growing body of research

    D   a genuine biological response

21. What does the writer tell us about Ader's and Evers' studies?

    A   Both involve gradually reducing the dosage of a drug.

    B   Evers is exploiting a response which Ader discovered by chance.

    C   Both examine the side effects caused by immunosuppressant drugs.

    D   Evers is investigating whether the human immune system reacts to placebos as Ader's rats did.

22. According to Charlotte Blease, placebos are omitted from medical training because

    A   there are so many practical subjects which need to be covered.

    B   those who train doctors do not believe that they work.

    C   they can be administered without specialist training.

    D   their effect is more psychological than physical.

END OF READING TEST
THIS BOOKLET WILL BE COLLECTED

WRITING SUB-TEST – TEST BOOKLET

CANDIDATE NUMBER:

LAST NAME:

FIRST NAME:

MIDDLE NAMES:

PROFESSION:

VENUE:

TEST DATE:

Candidate details and photo will be printed here.

Passport Photo

CANDIDATE DECLARATION

By signing this, you agree not to disclose or use in any way (other than to take the test) or assist any other person to disclose or use any OET test or sub-test content. If you cheat or assist in any cheating, use any unfair practice, break any of the rules or regulations, or ignore any advice or information, you may be disqualified and your results may not be issued at the sole discretion of CBLA. CBLA also reserves its right to take further disciplinary action against you and to pursue any other remedies permitted by law. If a candidate is suspected of and investigated for malpractice, their personal details and details of the investigation may be passed to a third party where required.

CANDIDATE SIGNATURE: _____

INSTRUCTIONS TO CANDIDATES

You must write your answer for the Writing sub-test in the **Writing Answer Booklet.**

You must **NOT** remove OET material from the test room.

www.occupationalenglishtest.org
© Cambridge Boxhill Language Assessment – ABN 51 988 559 414

[CANDIDATE NO.] WRITING SUB-TEST TEST BOOKLET 01/04

OCCUPATIONAL ENGLISH TEST

WRITING SUB-TEST: MEDICINE

TIME ALLOWED: READING TIME: 5 MINUTES
WRITING TIME: 40 MINUTES

Read the case notes below and complete the writing task which follows.

Notes:

You are a general practitioner. Ms Sarah Day, 21 years old, has been attending your practice since her early childhood.

Patient: Ms Sarah Day, D.O.B. 29.07.1997

Past medical history:
- **Jul 2001:** varicella
- **Apr 2002:** measles
- **Jan 2004:** fractured ulna
- **Jun 2006:** URTI
- **Sep 2008:** plantar warts
- **Dec 2011:** dysmenorrhoea
- **Apr 2013:** teenage acne
- **Aug 2014:** pre-menstrual syndrome
- **Jun 2015:** exam-related anxiety
- **Nov 2016:** oro-facial herpes simplex virus

Social background:
University student – not happy with course of study
Part-time job – McDonald's
Irregular hours, 5-8 hrs sleep/night
Smokes, drinks moderately
Lives at home with parents, boyfriend for 7 months

Medications: Oral contraceptive pill (prescribed April 2013) cyproterone acetate/ethinylestradiol – mane

06.12.18 Pt presented with mother complaining of unilateral headache – occipital, temporal extending to vertex, dizziness/loss of balance, with nausea and anxiety. Visual disturbances. Better when lying down. Symptoms not affected by red wine, alcohol, chocolate, cheese, sunlight. Not related to menstrual cycle or stress

Pt reports workload stress, pressure of assignments & exams

Episodes: x2 in past 2 weeks

Pain: Steady, not throbbing

Onset: Rapid
Aura
Symptoms last 1-2 days (severe for several hours)
No family history of headaches/migraines

Examination: No abnormal neurological signs

Treatment:	Education: rest/relaxation/meditation, adequate sleep, regular eating
	During attack: sleep, dark room, ice
	Metoclopramide 10 mg – orally → 20 mins later paracetamol 1 g – 4 hrly (max 4 g/24 hrs)
04.01.19	Attacks more frequent. Prescribed medications ineffective
	Pain felt in neck
	Anxiety becoming worse
	Dizziness during attacks
	Vomited on one occasion
	Mother reports Pt becoming afraid to leave house in case attack occurs
	No identifiable triggers
	Dark room, ice – no effect
Treatment:	Eletriptan 40 mg – orally on attack
	Ibuprofen 400 mg – 6 hrly (max t.d.s.)
31.01.19	Pt complained of drowsiness and diarrhoea since commenced on eletriptan
	No improvement in symptoms. Anxiety worse – Pt describes as 'panic' accompanying symptoms
	Mother concerned daughter becoming depressed: withdrawn, housebound, losing interest in usual activities & boyfriend, oversleeping, comfort eating → weight gain
	B.P 120/80
Treatment:	Amitriptyline 25 mg – b.d.
24.02.19	Pt presented alone. Complains of numbness and tingling (paraesthesia) in fingers 4 & 5 left hand No improvement in symptoms
	Pt reported car accident Jun 2017. Not previously disclosed as wishes to keep from mother. Sustained 'whiplash injury'
	No treatment sought at time
	Referral to neurologist, for investigation and management

Writing Task:

Using the information in the case notes, write a letter of referral to Dr Robert Edwards, a neurologist. Outline Ms Day's relevant history and request further investigations and management. Address the letter to Dr Robert Edwards, Rushford Hospital, 765 Long Gully Road, Littletown.

In your answer:
- **Expand the relevant notes into complete sentences**
- **Do not use note form**
- **Use letter format**

The body of the letter should be approximately 180–200 words.

WRITING SUB-TEST – ANSWER BOOKLET

CANDIDATE NUMBER:

LAST NAME:

FIRST NAME:

MIDDLE NAMES:

PROFESSION:

VENUE:

TEST DATE:

Candidate details and photo will be printed here.

Passport Photo

CANDIDATE DECLARATION

By signing this, you agree not to disclose or use in any way (other than to take the test) or assist any other person to disclose or use any OET test or sub-test content. If you cheat or assist in any cheating, use any unfair practice, break any of the rules or regulations, or ignore any advice or information, you may be disqualified and your results may not be issued at the sole discretion of CBLA. CBLA also reserves its right to take further disciplinary action against you and to pursue any other remedies permitted by law. If a candidate is suspected of and investigated for malpractice, their personal details and details of the investigation may be passed to a third party where required.

CANDIDATE SIGNATURE: _____

TIME ALLOWED
READING TIME: 5 MINUTES
WRITING TIME: 40 MINUTES

INSTRUCTIONS TO CANDIDATES

1. **Reading time: 5 minutes**
   During this time you may study the writing task and notes. You **MUST NOT** write, highlight, underline or make any notes.

2. **Writing time: 40 minutes**

3. Use the back page for notes and rough draft only. Notes and rough draft will **NOT** be marked.

   Please write your answer clearly on page 1 and page 2.

   Cross out anything you **DO NOT** want the examiner to consider.

4. You must write your answer for the Writing sub-test in this **Answer Booklet** using **pen or pencil**.

5. You must **NOT** remove OET material from the test room.

www.occupationalenglishtest.org
© Cambridge Boxhill Language Assessment – ABN 51 988 559 414

[CANDIDATE NO.] WRITING SUB-TEST ANSWER BOOKLET 01/04

Please record your answer on this page.

(Only answers on Page 1 and Page 2 will be marked.)

Please record your answer on this page.

(Only answers on Page 1 and Page 2 will be marked.)

OET Writing sub-test – Answer booklet 2

[CANDIDATE NO.] WRITING SUB-TEST - ANSWER BOOKLET 03/04

Space for notes and rough draft. Only your answers on Page 1 and Page 2 will be marked.

SPEAKING SUB-TEST

CANDIDATE NUMBER:

LAST NAME:

FIRST NAME:

MIDDLE NAMES:

PROFESSION: Your details and photo will be printed here.

VENUE:

TEST DATE:

Passport Photo

CANDIDATE DECLARATION

By signing this, you agree not to disclose or use in any way (other than to take the test) or assist any other person to disclose or use any OET test or sub-test content. If you cheat or assist in any cheating, use any unfair practice, break any of the rules or regulations, or ignore any advice or information, you may be disqualified and your results may not be issued at the sole discretion of CBLA. CBLA also reserves its right to take further disciplinary action against you and to pursue any other remedies permitted by law. If a candidate is suspected of and investigated for malpractice, their personal details and details of the investigation may be passed to a third party where required.

CANDIDATE SIGNATURE: _____

INSTRUCTION TO CANDIDATES

Please confirm with the Interlocutor that your roleplay card number and colour match the Interlocutor card before you begin.

Interlocutor to complete only

ID No: _____ Passport: ☐   National ID: ☐   Alternative ID approved: ☐

Speaking sub-test:

ID document sighted? ☐   Photo match? ☐   Signature match? ☐   Did not attend? ☐

Interlocutor name: _____

Interlocutor signature: _____

www.occupationalenglishtest.org
© Cambridge Boxhill Language Assessment – ABN 51 988 559 414
[CANDIDATE NO.] SPEAKING SUB-TEST 01/04

OET Sample role-play

ROLEPLAYER CARD NO. 1 — MEDICINE

SETTING Suburban General Practice

PATIENT You are 45 years old and have had a cold for the past five days. You have come to the doctor because this morning you noticed an unusual rash on the left side of your chest. The rash consists of a series of tiny blisters in a small cluster along the skin over your fifth rib. The rash is becoming increasingly itchy and sore. You have been otherwise well recently, and have no other medical problems. You had chickenpox during childhood.

TASK
- Explain your current symptoms: Your cold symptoms (runny nose and sore throat) are actually getting better, but you are now concerned about the rash because it is quite itchy and painful. You would like to know what this rash is, and what you should be doing about it.

- Be anxious and demand a lot of reassurance from the doctor about the origin of the rash and what will happen to you. (Is it related to my recent cold? Is it related to some other illness or is something else wrong with me? How long will I have this rash? Can't something be done to take it away quickly? Will it spread all over my body?)

© Cambridge Boxhill Language Assessment   Sample role-play

OET Sample role-play

CANDIDATE CARD NO. 1 — MEDICINE

SETTING Suburban General Practice

DOCTOR This 45-year-old patient presents with a five-day history of simple upper respiratory symptoms. This morning he/she noticed a vesicular rash on the upper left chest wall, on the skin over the fifth rib. On examination, the ears and throat are normal, and the rash has the classic appearance of herpes zoster. Other results of the physical examination are normal. The patient is otherwise in excellent health. He/she had chickenpox in childhood.

TASK
- Find out about the patient's current symptoms.
- Explain your diagnosis – a mild case of shingles – and the probable cause. (The patient's recent cold has weakened resistance, but another virus, the herpes zoster or chickenpox virus, is causing the skin spots.)
- Suggest treatment to reduce pain (e.g., a topical cream, oral pain relief such as paracetamol if the pain is severe enough, etc.).
- Find out what will reassure the patient. Mention that the rash usually fades by itself over several weeks, though even a small outbreak can be uncomfortable.
- Advise the patient to return if the rash spreads, or if simple measures fail to contain the symptoms.
- Reassure the patient that this condition does not imply other illness or abnormality, and that spread is unlikely.

© Cambridge Boxhill Language Assessment   Sample role-play

OET Sample role-play

ROLEPLAYER CARD NO. 2   **MEDICINE**

SETTING   Suburban General Practice

PARENT   You have brought your two-year-old son to see the doctor. He is your only child. His general health has been good and he has had no significant illnesses previously.

TASK
- When asked, explain that your child's appetite has been poor, he never finishes his plate of food, and he dislikes many foods. He drinks plenty of milk and sweet, sugary drinks. Find out why your child is eating so poorly. You are worried about his weight
- Ask if he needs tests to determine the nature of the problem.
- Find out if there's anything you can you do to improve his appetite. You don't want to decrease the amount of milk and sweet, sugary drinks he consumes as you are worried that then he won't eat anything.
- Don't be easily reassured.
- Accept the doctor's advice.

© Cambridge Boxhill Language Assessment   Sample role-play

OET Sample role-play

CANDIDATE CARD NO. 2   **MEDICINE**

SETTING   Suburban General Practice

DOCTOR   This concerned parent has brought his/her two-year-old son to see you. He has no significant medical history and is otherwise well.

TASK
- Find out the patient's signs (behaviour) and any other relevant dietary information.
- Explain that the child appears perfectly healthy and is a normal weight and height for his age.
- Explain that food refusal is quite common at this age, and the amount of food required is less when the child is not in a phase of rapid growth.
- Discuss the amount of milk and sugary drinks the child is drinking and suggest decreasing this intake.
- Offer to review the child and re-measure him in four weeks.

© Cambridge Boxhill Language Assessment   Sample role-play

Listening sub-test
ANSWER KEY – Parts A, B & C

LISTENING SUB-TEST – ANSWER KEY

PART A: QUESTIONS 1-12

1 dry

2 (very) gradual

3 swollen / bulging (out)

4 soft

5 farm labourer

6 (night) security guard

7 beta blockers

8 crackling (accept: cracking)/ crep / crepitation

9 (bad) eczema

10 echocardiogram / cardiac echo / echo

11 arterial blood gas / ABG

12 corticosteroids

PART A: QUESTIONS 13-24

13 myopic / short(-)sighted / near(-)sighted

14 nystagmus / (a) flicker(ing)

15 pigment (in eye)

16 driving

17 focus

18 distance

19 (hotel) receptionist

20 cataract (developed)

21 opacity / clouding

22 detached retina / retina(l) detachment

23 (eye) floaters

24 glare / bright lights

LISTENING SUB-TEST – ANSWER KEY

PART B: QUESTIONS 25-30

25	A	remove her saline drip
26	C	relatively high staff absence rates
27	C	prepare to cope with an increasing demand for it.
28	B	Nobody has taken responsibility for assessing the patient.
29	B	expand upon what they studied previously.
30	C	warning him about a possible problem

PART C: QUESTIONS 31-36

31	B	Their condition can develop in a number of different ways.
32	A	There was a lack of reliable information on it.
33	B	was more widely available than some users imagined.
34	C	may lead to dementia patients experiencing unnecessary distress.
35	A	illustrate a gap in current medical education programmes.
36	B	it avoids carers having to speculate about a patient's wishes.

PART C: QUESTIONS 37-42

37	B	observing the effects of poor communication on a patient.
38	A	The information given can overwhelm patients.
39	C	relatives' knowledge of a patient's condition shouldn't be taken for granted.
40	A	measured the difference between their expectations and their actual experience.
41	B	the over-use of unclear medical terminology with patients.
42	A	surprised by one response from patients

END OF KEY

Listening sub-test
Audio Script – Practice test 3

OCCUPATIONAL ENGLISH TEST. PRACTICE TEST 2. LISTENING TEST.

This test has three parts. In each part you'll hear a number of different extracts. At the start of each extract, you'll hear this sound: ---***---.

You'll have time to read the questions before you hear each extract and you'll hear each extract ONCE only. Complete your answers as you listen.

At the end of the test, you'll have two minutes to check your answers.

Part A. In this part of the test, you'll hear two different extracts. In each extract, a health professional is talking to a patient. For questions 1 to 24, complete the notes with information you hear. Now, look at the notes for extract one.

PAUSE: 5 SECONDS
Extract one. Questions 1 to 12.

You hear a consultant endocrinologist talking to a patient called Sarah Croft. For questions 1 to 12, complete the notes with a word or short phrase. You now have thirty seconds to look at the notes.

PAUSE: 30 SECONDS
---***---

You hear a pulmonologist talking to a patient called Robert Miller. For questions 1 to 12, complete the notes with a word or short phrase. You now have thirty seconds to look at the notes.

PAUSE: 30 SECONDS
---***---

F   Good morning, Mr Miller. Now, looking at your notes, I see you've been having a few problems recently. Could you tell me a little about what's been happening, in your own words?

M   Well, yeah – it's a combination of things really. To kick-off, I feel pretty tired most of the time – just haven't got the energy I used to have. And I've got this cough – it's there all the time and it feels dry – I mean, I'm not coughing up phlegm or blood or anything like that. But the worst thing, which really bothers me, is that I'm so short of breath – even if I'm just getting dressed in the morning or going up a few steps, I have to stop 'cos I get breathless so quickly. And I've lost quite a bit of weight, too – I mean, I didn't notice at first cos it was very gradual. But all in all, I'm about ten kilos lighter than I was six months ago. I've not been dieting or anything – I, I love my food!

F   OK. And, well have you noticed anything else?

M   Yeah – just take a look at my fingers. The tips look swollen, don't they – and it's the same with my toes, which are bulging out at the end too. It's weird. And my nails – I don't understand it – they've become soft. They're not hard like they used to be. Look....

F   Erm, OK ... I see what you mean. And tell me a little about yourself.... Umm what do you do for a living?

M   Well, till recently, I worked as a farm labourer. Did it for about twenty years in total. It was hard physical graft, and it finally got to the stage where I just couldn't cope with it any more. It really took it out of me. So, this last couple of years, I've been a security guard, working nights at a local DIY warehouse. It's a bit boring, and the late shifts took a bit of getting used to, but it's OK.

F   And, erm, are you finding it less physically demanding?

M   That's right. I just haven't got the stamina now for anything else – in fact, I've even had to give up my golf. Can't manage it any more. Any spare time now goes on looking after my pigeons – I've done that since I was a teenager.

F   Oh very nice. And, erm, what about your medical history. Now, I see you were diagnosed with hypertension last year, and you're taking beta blockers at the moment for that.

M   That's right. My GP said it'd help. Something the GP also said, when I saw him about my breathing problems, was that he heard what he called 'crackling' noises in my chest. I can't hear them, but he could - through the stethoscope.

F   OK. And is there any family history of breathing or lung problems, or any serious illnesses that you know of?

M   I don't think so. My mother was always healthy, but my dad developed bad eczema as an adult. I remember the red patches on his hands and face. But he didn't have any lung problems as far as I know.

F   Right, and… well looking at your previous tests, you were diagnosed with hypertension about 6 months ago, you had…

M   Oh yeah, erm… an echocardiogram, you know, to check my heart… and a chest x-ray about four weeks ago after I saw my GP. That came back OK as far as I know.

F   I see.

M   I'm not keen on hospitals, to be honest. Am I going to need to have lots more tests?

F   Well, I'm going to suggest you have what's called an arterial blood gas test. This will let us check how well your lungs are working – how they move oxygen into your blood and remove carbon dioxide from it.

M   OK.

F   And, I'm also going to order a CT scan. Now, this'll be more revealing than the chest x-ray you had. And I may then prescribe a course of corticosteroids. This will depend on what the tests show up. Now, I'd start you on a relatively low dose and then we'll … [fade]

PAUSE: 10 SECONDS
Extract two. Questions 13 to 24.

You hear an eye specialist talking to a patient called Jasmine Burton, who has recently undergone eye surgery. For questions 13 to 24, complete the notes with a word or short phrase. You now have thirty seconds to look at the notes.

PAUSE: 30 SECONDS
---***---

M: I've got your notes here Mrs Burton, but as we're meeting for the first time, could you begin by telling me a little about your eyesight and the treatment you've had over the years. Erm, did you wear glasses as a child, for example?

F: Ahh yes, since I was about seven. My parents were concerned by the way I held a book when I was reading so they took me to an optometrist. He told them I had some kind of astigmatism.

M: Am I right in assuming that's myopic rather than hyperopic?

F: *Well yes, I'm near-sighted…if that's what you mean.*

M: That's right. Some people actually have mixed astigmatism - they're far-sighted in one eye and near in the other.

F: *Oh well, that's not me. And, as well as my astigmatism, as you've probably noticed, my eyes flicker. I'm not aware of it myself but other people comment on it sometimes. I think you call it…nystagmus. It meant that, when I had my eye surgery, they preferred to use a general rather than a local anaesthetic.*

M: OK, so did anyone ever tell you what they thought might have caused the condition?

F: *Well, I was once told that my generally poor eyesight is most probably down to the fact that I don't have enough pigment in the eye. On the whole, my eyes have never really caused me any significant difficulties, however. I've always had to wear glasses, so that's a part of life now. I suppose…the only thing is that driving's always been out of the question. I'd never have passed the sight part of the test. That's probably a good thing because it takes me some time to focus, which could make me pretty dangerous if I was ever behind the wheel of a car.*

M: Yes, indeed.

F: *Also I'm useless at sports like tennis - I think that's because I'm…I'm poor at judging the distance between myself and the ball. That was a pain as a teenager, but I've never particularly wanted to play since then. And I've hardly had any issues at work because of my sight. I'm a receptionist in a hotel and I've never had any difficulty reading computer screens or anything fortunately.*

M: You've…You've had your eyes regularly checked throughout your life presumably?

F: *Yeah that's right. Every couple of years. My prescription's changed a little over time - but not that much. Though I certainly couldn't manage without reading glasses these days. About three years ago, I was told a cataract was developing in my right eye. It was a few years before they decided to remove it – that was this February – and it all went very smoothly.*

M: Good, and you… you were pleased with the result?

F: *Yeah I was, yeah, thrilled. If only all our failing parts could be replaced so easily! However, when I had the routine check-up a couple of weeks after the operation, I was told there was some clouding…err opacity, I think was the word they used - in the capsule containing the new lens. It's a bit disappointing. They could clear it with a laser if it gets to be a real problem…erm, but my flicker makes that rather a risky option. I knew that there's a greater chance of developing a detached retina after a cataract op…but I'm glad to say they found there wasn't any evidence of that in my case. All they did was make an appointment for me to be checked out again in six months-time. But they said I should get in touch if I felt concerned about my eyes.*

M: And is that what brings you here today?

F: *Yeah, because I am bothered about a couple of things. So, firstly I've noticed more floaters than usual. I don't know if that's something to worry about or not. Erm, more annoying is the fact that I'm much more troubled by glare than I used to be. So I wanted to ask your opinion on that.*

M: OK, well let's start by having …..[fade]

PAUSE: 10 SECONDS
That is the end of Part A. Now, look at Part B.

PAUSE: 5 SECONDS

Part B. In this part of the test, you'll hear six different extracts. In each extract, you'll hear people talking in a different healthcare setting.

For questions 25 to 30, choose the answer A, B or C which fits best according to what you hear. You'll have time to read each question before you listen. Complete your answers as you listen.

Now look at Question 25. You hear a nurse briefing a colleague at the end of her shift. Now read the question.

PAUSE: 15 SECONDS
---***---

F   OK, so the next thing is about Suzie Williams in bed three.

M   Right.

F   She's been admitted for chest pain to rule out MI. So far she had an EKG which was OK, and the first set of cardiac enzymes and troponins are negative. When she came in, her blood pressure was elevated a little, like one eighty two over ninety five, but she was given losartan and at six o'clock it was one forty two over eighty two. She was also dehydrated so we started her on IV fluids, D5 half-normal saline running at a hundred and twenty five millilitres. That can go until midnight and then it can be disconnected. She's scheduled for a stress test tomorrow and some more enzyme tests. OK?

M   OK.

PAUSE: 5 SECONDS
Question 26. You hear part of a hospital management meeting where a concern is being discussed. Now read the question.

PAUSE: 15 SECONDS
---***---

M   Now I'll hand over to Jenny, who has a few words to say about staffing. Jenny?

F   Thanks. Now, if we compare ourselves to other hospitals of the same size, in other regions, we're actually recording lower rates of staff turnover. That's just as well given the challenges filling vacant positions across the sector. Where we do compare unfavourably is in the number of days lost to sick leave. That's making it hard to maintain full cover on the wards, and we all know the costs of that. As a matter of urgency then, HR are looking into the worst affected areas to understand the reasons behind it and to see if there's anything we can do to help and support the staff involved.

PAUSE: 5 SECONDS
Question 27. You hear a GP and his practice nurse discussing a vaccination programme. Now read the question.

192   PRACTICE TEST 3   ANSWER KEYS

PAUSE: 15 SECONDS
---***---

M: It's coming up to that time of year when we have to start preparing for the flu vaccination programme.

F: Yes, we usually do it at the start of next month, don't we?

M: That's right. If you remember last year we hired a local hall and did as many people as we could in one afternoon.

F: Yes, I'd just started working here then. It was a hectic couple of hours but it worked pretty well, don't you think?

M: Sure, but there's been so much publicity recently about how sensible it is to get the jab that I suspect we'll have a lot more people coming along this year.

F: So we better think about taking on an agency nurse perhaps to lend an extra hand.

M: OK. Let's run that by the practice manager. And she might have some other suggestions too.

PAUSE: 5 SECONDS
Question 28. You hear two hospital nurses discussing the assessment of a patient on their ward. Now read the question.

PAUSE: 15 SECONDS
---***---

M The bed manager just rang. He wants us to clear three spaces in the ward. Today.

F Oh it's never-ending! Let's see what we can do. There's no one ready to be discharged. But we could try chasing referrals for Mr Davison to the community hospital for rehab. Where are his notes?

M Yes, but has he had his assessment yet?

F They were all away at that conference yesterday and the day before. I think he'll have slipped through the net.

M: But Doctor Ammat's already got him medically stable and signed off. So he should be the next one to move on.

F Well I'd get him there as quickly as possible before they give the place to somebody else.

M I'll phone them straight away.

PAUSE: 5 SECONDS
Question 29. You hear the beginning of a training session for dental students. Now read the question.

PAUSE: 15 SECONDS
---***---

F This is session number four, which is going to include, again, impression-taking. We've created the crown impression of tooth number 30, we also took care of an inlay preparation. So today we're going to stay on that side with our impression-taking. We're going to make a duplicate of what we've already done. And our attention to detail is now going up another notch.

When I take an impression of a tooth that I've created in the mouth, I naturally have to take care of the saliva, the blood, the gum tissue… We're not going to cover all that today. You'll hit that next semester. What we are going to cover are the dynamics of your impression, the margins, the proximal contacts, the bite and the occlusion. We're going to capture all that in one impression.

PAUSE: 5 SECONDS

Question 30. You hear two nurses discussing the treatment of a patient with a kidney infection. Now read the question.

PAUSE: 15 SECONDS

---***---

M   I can't see the results of Mr Roberts' last blood test to check creatinine levels. Did you do the last one?

F   No, not me. Let's see. Ah, here it is. The last test was four hours ago and results show a level of thirty eight, so it's still well below normal. We'd better do one when he wakes up, as it might have changed. The patient's not keen on needles though. I had a real job last night trying to convince him it was necessary. Not the easiest of patients, if you're happy to have
a go.

M   OK. My turn, I reckon.

PAUSE: 10 SECONDS
That is the end of Part B. Now, look at Part C.

PAUSE: 5 SECONDS

Part C. In this part of the test, you'll hear two different extracts. In each extract, you'll hear health professionals talking about aspects of their work.

For questions 31 to 42, choose the answer A, B or C which fits best according to what you hear. Complete your answers as you listen.

Now look at extract one.

Extract one. Questions 31 to 36. You hear a geriatrician called Dr Clare Cox giving a presentation on the subject of end-of-life care for people with dementia.

You now have 90 seconds to read questions 31 to 36.

PAUSE: 90 SECONDS

---***---

F: My name's Dr Clare Cox. I'm a geriatrician specialising in palliative care. My topic today is an increasingly important issue: end-of-life care for dementia patients.

The care of dementia patients presents certain problems. Dementia is a terminal illness and is the third highest cause of death in Australia. But dementia is different from other such conditions. It has an unpredictable trajectory and there can be difficult issues around patients' mental capacity, decision-making and communication. But, in spite of an equal need for palliative care services, dementia patients don't always fit the traditional model of such care. Families often suffer distress because they feel unable to ensure that their loved one's wishes are being respected, or just don't know what that person wanted because the discussion wasn't held early enough. There is, therefore, a clear need for well-funded, patient-centred palliative dementia care that's available when and where it's needed.

I do a lot of work with Dementia Australia – an organisation which represents the needs of Australians living with all types of dementia, and of their families and carers. It also campaigns on dementia issues and funds research.

Dementia Australia decided it was the right time to examine the issue of end-of-life dementia care, from the perspective of the consumer as well as from that of the healthcare professional. It's a timely initiative. We have plenty of anecdotal evidence, but not enough hard facts about what's going wrong and why the system's failing. But the current situation isn't all bad. Despite the issues I've mentioned, I've heard some wonderful examples of how palliative care has made a big difference to people's lives. Things can obviously go badly wrong if this isn't handled well, but in the right circumstances people with dementia can reach the end of their lives peacefully and with dignity.

Dementia Australia commissioned researchers to conduct a survey on the end-of-life issues affecting dementia patients. The survey covered both care professionals, that's doctors, nurses and others working with dementia patients, as well as family-member carers. The interest was overwhelming with more than a thousand responses from around Australia. But what do the results tell us? Well, the initial results confirmed what we've heard about access to appropriate end-of-life care. It was obvious immediately that there was a striking gap between the perceptions of care professionals, and family-member carers about end-of-life dementia care. For instance, while fifty-eight per cent of family-member carers said that they didn't have access to palliative care specialists, and sixty-eight per cent didn't have access to hospices, three-quarters of care professionals indicated that people with dementia in their area do in fact have access to palliative care. This begs the question of whether consumers – that is patients and family-member carers – might not be aware of services that are available.

Another notable finding of the survey was that care professionals often lack knowledge of the legal issues surrounding end-of-life care. Some reports indicate that care professionals are at times reluctant to use pain medications such as morphine because of concerns about hastening a patient's death. However, access to appropriate pain relief is considered to be a fundamental human right, even if death is earlier as a secondary effect of medication. Our survey found that twenty-seven per cent of care professionals were unsure about this, or didn't believe that patients are legally entitled to adequate pain control, if it might hasten death. So perhaps it isn't surprising then, that a quarter of former family-member carers felt that pain wasn't adequately managed in end-of-life care.

This lack of awareness extends beyond pain management. The statistics on refusing treatment were particularly shocking. Almost a third of care professionals were unaware that people have the right to refuse food and hydration, and one in ten also thought refusal of antibiotics wasn't an option for patients in end-of-life care. How can we ever achieve consumer empowerment and consumer-directed care if the professionals are so ill informed? There's a clear need for greater information and training on patient rights, yet over a third of care professionals said they hadn't received any such training at all.

It's obvious that end-of-life care planning is desirable. Discussing and documenting preferences is clearly the best way of minimising the burden of decision-making on carers, and ensuring patients' wishes are respected. Advance care planning is essentially an insurance policy that helps to protect our patients in case they lose their decision-making capacity. Even though a patient might believe that loved ones will have their best interests at heart, the evidence shows that such people aren't that good at knowing what decisions those they love would make on complex matters such as infection control and hydration.

So, before I go on to …..[fade]

PAUSE: 10 SECONDS

Now look at extract two.

Extract two. Questions 37 to 42. You hear a hospital doctor called Dr Keith Gardiner giving a presentation about some research he's done on the subject of staff-patient communication.

You now have 90 seconds to read questions 37 to 42.

PAUSE: 90 SECONDS

---***---

M: Good morning. My name's Dr Keith Gardiner, and I'd like to talk to you today about some research I've been involved in, concerning something that affects all health professionals – staff-patient communication.

Now, firstly, let me reassure you that in feedback, patients seem positive about the way information is communicated to them. But I recently decided to explore the issue in more detail when I was in a hospital with a patient and witnessed for myself what can result when a health care professional assumes they've made themselves clear to a patient, when in fact they've been anything but. Luckily, I've had very few complaints made against members of my team, but the potential is certainly there.

So first, let's start by looking at a typical hospital admission for an in-patient, and the first communication they have about any procedures they are to undergo. On arrival, a patient will complete necessary paperwork. Various staff will talk to them about their treatment during their stay, which is designed to reduce patient anxiety. However, from some patients' point of view, this interaction can seem very complex and difficult to take in, especially at a time when they're not at their best physically or mentally. So it's doubly important to check that any communication has been understood.

Now, to illustrate what I'm talking about, let's take a hypothetical situation. I often use this because it highlights the potential consequences of poor communication. A man in his eighties is admitted to hospital, despite his protestations, with ongoing severe back pain. On investigation, it's found his cancer has spread. The outlook is poor - and further compounded by his becoming depressed and refusing to eat while in hospital. A feeding tube is inserted, a procedure which the patient complies with, but which his family members query. The doctor on duty updates them, assuming they're aware of the severity of the patient's condition – when in fact no such prognosis has been shared with them. An extreme case, but a plausible one, nevertheless.

In order to find out exactly what in-patients felt about the service they were receiving in this hospital, we conducted a patient survey. The questions were carefully targeted to capture patients' opinions about the effectiveness of the communication they'd been involved in during their stay. The survey questioned patients on both what they had expected prior to admission, and what their stay was really like. These two scores were then used to calculate what's called a 'gap' score. The survey also included questions to measure the patients' behavioural intention – that is, how willing they would be to return to the hospital for treatment. Patients completed the survey themselves, and results were then processed with the help of medical students.

Now, the survey produced some interesting data about communication, including both praise and complaints. Clearly in a hospital situation, staff are dealing with confidential and sensitive information, which must be communicated in private – a situation which can be difficult to achieve in a large and busy hospital. However, we scored highly on that point. And we were also pleased to note that staff did manage to communicate in a manner that treated patients with dignity and respect. Of course, staff also have to ensure patients fully understand what's been said to them. And this last point's where we received the most negative feedback. Both patients and relatives noted a tendency for professionals to resort to the use of jargon, and complex terms when explaining both diagnoses and procedures, which left some patients confused. However, patients were generally satisfied with the information about any follow-up treatment provided after discharge.

Also, once we'd sifted through all the results, a clear pattern began to emerge regarding the care given by nurses, which I found particularly interesting. I'd assumed that having a number of different nurses attending to a patient during their stay was a good thing, because you need enough staff to cover the various shifts, and attend to patients' needs. What I certainly hadn't expected, though, was for patients to say they felt their recovery was faster when they had to communicate with only a small number of nurses - in other words when they were surrounded by familiar faces. The findings aren't conclusive, and more investigative work needs to be done on a bigger sample – but it's certainly food for thought.

PAUSE: 10 SECONDS
That is the end of Part C.

You now have two minutes to check your answers.

PAUSE: 120 SECONDS
That is the end of the Listening test.

Reading sub-test

Answer Key – Part A

READING SUB-TEST – ANSWER KEY

PART A: QUESTIONS 1-20

1	B
2	A
3	C
4	D
5	C
6	B
7	D
8	clindamycin (and) penicillin
9	diabetes mellitus
10	septic shock
11	VAC/ vacuum-assisted closure
12	alcohol pads
13	daptomycin (and) linezolid
14	vibrio (infection)
15	32.2%
16	seafood
17	limbs
18	polymicrobial
19	7%
20	physical therapy

Reading sub-test
Answer Key – Parts B & C

READING SUB-TEST – ANSWER KEY

PART B: QUESTIONS 1-6

1	A	stop dates aren't relevant in all circumstances.
2	B	improves precision during radiation.
3	B	position electrodes correctly.
4	C	its short-term benefits are explained to them.
5	B	the use of a particular method of testing pH levels.
6	A	the amount of oxytocin given will depend on how the patient reacts.

PART C: QUESTIONS 7-14

7	D	the need for the phobia to be confronted repeatedly over time.
8	D	unpleasant memories are aroused in response to certain prompts.
9	A	makes use of an innate function of the brain.
10	A	the anxiety that patients feel during therapy
11	C	affects how neurons in the brain react to stimuli.
12	A	its benefits are likely to be of limited duration.
13	D	the emotional force of a memory is naturally retained.
14	B	increase patients' tolerance of key triggers.

PART C: QUESTIONS 15-22

15	A	he saw for himself how it could work in practice.
16	A	research indicates that they are effective even without deceit.
17	D	they are very widely used
18	A	The way a treatment is presented is significant even if it is a placebo.
19	B	reduce the number of people who experience them.
20	C	a growing body of research
21	B	Evers is exploiting a response which Ader discovered by chance.
22	D	their effect is more psychological than physical.

OCCUPATIONAL ENGLISH TEST

WRITING SUB-TEST: MEDICINE

SAMPLE RESPONSE: LETTER OF REFERRAL

Dr Robert Edwards
Rushford Hospital
765 Long Gully Road
Littletown

24 February 2019

Re: Ms Sarah Day (DOB: 29.07.1997)

Dear Dr Edwards,

Thank you for seeing Ms Day, a 21-year-old university student, for investigation and management of recent headaches.

Ms Day has a three-month history of episodic unilateral steady headaches (occipitotemporal extending to vertex) accompanied by loss of balance, nausea and worsening anxiety. In January, she also reported neck pain. The symptoms are becoming more frequent and have not responded to migraine treatments (dark room, sleep and ice). The usual triggers and ameliorating factors for migraine are absent.

Today, she also complained of paraesthesia (numbness and tingling) in fingers 4 and 5 of her left hand. Ms Day has recently disclosed that, in June 2017, she was involved in a car accident in which she sustained a whiplash injury. No treatment was sought at that time.

Initial management of her headaches included metoclopramide 10 mg and paracetamol 1 g. Subsequent medications prescribed were eletriptan 40 mg at the commencement of an attack, with ibuprofen 400 mg on 04/01/19. Ms Day reported experiencing drowsiness and diarrhoea after commencing eletriptan. Amitriptyline 25 mg twice a day was prescribed on 31/01/19. Her only other current medication is cyproterone acetate/ethinylestradiol mane.

If you require any further information, please do not hesitate to contact me.

Yours sincerely,

Doctor

How we assess Writing

OET is a test of English language, not a test of professional knowledge.

The candidate's writing performance in the single writing task is assessed by two qualified assessors who have been trained in OET assessment procedures.

The Writing task responses are assessed in Melbourne, Australia. All responses are double marked.

Subject matter experts for each profession are involved in the test writing process and identify the key relevant information from the case notes which must be included in responses for the reader to be adequately informed. The assessors are language experts trained to assess how this information is communicated.

Rationale

In the healthcare workplace, professionals are expected to be able to communicate with colleagues, peers and patients clearly and effectively. The Writing task allows candidates to demonstrate the ability to communicate information about a healthcare scenario in written form.

The case notes provided in the Writing task present candidates with authentic stimulus material from which to demonstrate their communicative writing proficiency.

The written letter task is designed to give candidates opportunities to demonstrate their communicative language ability in ways that are valued in the healthcare context.

For example, that they can:

» summarise information about a patient or healthcare situation to provide the reader with the salient points.
» select and prioritise information which is relevant to the reader.
» make requests for action to ensure continuity of care.
» communicate information using appropriate formality and language as would be expected from someone working in the healthcare field.

The candidate's performance in the written task is assessed against 6 criteria:

1. Purpose (3 marks)
2. Content
3. Conciseness & Clarity
4. Genre & Style   (7 marks each)
5. Organisation & Layout
6. Language

Your letter is assessed against six criteria:

» **Purpose:** Whether the purpose of the letter is immediately apparent to the reader and sufficiently expanded in the course of the letter.
» **Content:** Whether all the necessary information is included and is accurate for the reader.
» **Conciseness & Clarity:** Whether unnecessary information is omitted so that the letter is an effective summary for the reader.
» **Genre & Style:** Whether the register, tone and use of abbreviations are appropriate for the reader.
» **Organisation & Layout:** Whether the letter is organised and well laid out for the reader.
» **Language:** Whether the accuracy of the grammar, vocabulary, spelling and punctuation communicates the necessary information to the reader.

MEDICINE

Purpose
- Clearly explain the main purpose of your letter early in the document, within the first paragraph when appropriate – this provides the context for the information you include.
- Clearly expand on the purpose within the letter – this assists the reader to understand what is required of them.
- Be clear about the level of urgency for the communication.

Content
- Always keep in mind the reason for writing – don't just summarise the case notes provided.
- Focus on important information and minimise incidental detail.
- Demonstrate in your response that you have understood the case notes fully.
- Be clear what the most relevant issues for the reader are.
- Don't let the main issue become hidden by including too much supporting detail.
- Show clearly the connections between information in the case notes if these are made; however, do not add information that is not given in the notes (e.g., your suggested diagnosis), particularly if the reason for the letter is to get an expert opinion.
- Take relevant information from the case notes and transform it to fit the task set.
- If the stimulus material includes questions that require an answer in your response, be explicit about this – don't 'hide' the relevant information in a general summary of the notes provided.
- Write enough so the reader would be accurately informed of the situation.

Conciseness & Clarity
- Avoid writing too much – if you select the case notes carefully, you will naturally end up within the guided word limit.
- Avoid using a 'formulaic' response – if you include elements that do not fit the task, it indicates a lack of flexibility in your writing.
- Don't include information that the intended reader clearly knows already (e.g., if you are replying to a colleague who has referred a patient to you).
- Don't include information that the reader will not need to provide continued care (e.g. medical history that is not relevant to the current situation).
- Use your own words to clearly summarise the case notes to keep information concise for the reader.

Genre & Style
- Remember that all professional letters are written in a relatively formal style.
- Avoid informal language, slang, colloquialisms and spoken idioms unless you are sure this is appropriate (e.g., use 'Thank you' rather than 'Thanks a lot').
- Avoid SMS texting abbreviations in a formal letter (e.g., use 'you' not 'u').
- Give the correct salutation: if you are told the recipient's name and title, use them.
- Show awareness of your audience by choosing appropriate words and phrases: if you are writing to another healthcare professional in the same medical discipline, you may use technical terms and, possibly, abbreviations. If you are writing to a parent or a group of lay people, use non-technical terms and explain carefully.
- Avoid judgemental or opinionated language. Clinical/factual language sounds more professional.
- Use short forms appropriately
  - Don't use symbols in formal letters.
  - Be judicious with your use of abbreviations. Use them minimally where a colleague would understand them but do not overuse so that the tone of your letter becomes informal.
- Use statements rather than questions to make requests (e.g. 'A second opinion would be appreciated' rather than 'Please can you provide a second opinion?') to explain action you want the reader to take.

- » Prioritise the patient or the treatment over who provided or authorised this treatment in the appropriate context (e.g., 'IV Morphine was commenced post-operatively' rather than 'I commenced the patient on IV Morphine post-operatively').
- » Refer to the patient by name not as 'the patient' or 'the client' to make your letter personalized and to sound polite. For children aged 16 years or younger, using their first name only is often appropriate following the initial introduction.
- » Remember brackets are not a common feature of formal writing and can often be replaced by a pair of commas or embedded within the sentence (e.g. 'have not responded to migraine treatments: dark room, sleep and ice' rather than 'have not responded to migraine treatments [dark room, sleep and ice]').
- » Close the letter using an appropriately formal salutation (e.g. 'Yours sincerely' or 'Yours faithfully' rather than 'Kind regards').

Organisation & Layout

- » Organise the information clearly – the sequence of information in the case notes may not be the most appropriate sequence of information for your letter.
- » Consider using dates and other time references (e.g., three months later, last week, a year ago, etc.) to give a clear sequence of events where necessary.
- » Think about your reader; writing about related information in the same paragraph is much clearer to understand
- » Use connecting words and phrases ('connectives') to link ideas together clearly (e.g., however, therefore, subsequently, etc.).
- » Use a clear layout to avoid any miscommunication: leave a blank line between paragraphs to show clearly the overall structure of the letter.
- » Avoid creating any negative impact on your reader through the presentation of the letter: don't write on every other line – this does not assist the reader particularly.
- » There is no need to include the patient's address as a separate part of your letter, you are not assessed on this.

Language

- » Show that you can use language accurately and flexibly in your writing.
- » Use language naturally – complex as well as simple sentences, a variety of tenses – to help your reader clearly understand the content.
- » Split a long sentence into two or three sentences if you feel you are losing control of it.
- » Review areas of grammar to ensure you convey your intended meaning accurately – particular areas to focus on might include*:
    - articles – a/an, the (e.g., 'She had an operation.', 'on the Internet')
    - countable and uncountable nouns (e.g., some evidence, an opinion, an asthma attack)
    - verb forms used to indicate past time and the relationship between events in the past and now (past simple, present perfect, past perfect)
    - adverbs that give time references (e.g., 'two months previously' is different from 'two months ago')
    - prepositions following other words (e.g., 'Thank you very much ~~to see~~ for seeing ...', 'sensitivity ~~of~~ to pressure', 'my examination ~~on~~ of the patient', 'diagnosed with cancer')
    - passive forms (e.g., '~~He involved in an accident.~~' for 'He was involved in an accident.')
- » Take care with the placement of commas and full stops:
    - Make sure there are enough – separating ideas into sentences.
    - Make sure there are not too many – keeping elements of the text meaningfully connected together.
    - Use as part of titles, dates and salutations if you prefer or omit if this is your personal style.

MEDICINE

How we assess Speaking

OET is a test of English language, not a test of professional knowledge.

The whole Speaking sub-test is audio recorded and the audio recording is assessed. The assessment is given on the candidate's performance in the two role-plays only (not the warm-up conversation).

The candidate's speaking performance is assessed by two qualified assessors who have been trained in OET assessment procedures.

The Speaking sub-test recordings are assessed in Melbourne, Australia. All recordings are double marked.

Important: The interlocutor is trained to ensure the structure of the Speaking sub-test is consistent for each candidate. The interlocutor also uses detailed information on his/her role-play card. The interlocutor DOES NOT assess the candidate.

Rationale

An important part of a health professional's role is the ability to communicate effectively in speech with his/her patients or clients. The role-plays allow the candidate to take his/her professional role and demonstrate the ability to deal with common workplace situations. These situations may include elements of tension which are a normal part of the real-life context, for example, anxious or angry patients, patients who misunderstand their situation, etc.

The two role-plays, each with a different scenario, provide two separate opportunities for the candidate to demonstrate spoken proficiency, therefore giving a broad view of the candidate's spoken skills.

Role-play tasks are designed to give candidates opportunities to demonstrate their language ability, for example, to:

- negotiate meaning with the interlocutor who is playing the role of the patient (e.g., reassure a worried patient, clarify a medical explanation, manage an upset patient, etc.).
- explain medical conditions/treatments and terminology in an accessible way.
- rephrase ideas and opinions in different ways to try and convince a patient.
- ask and answer questions to and from the patient.
- engage with a variety of patient types (different ages, personalities, different health concerns, etc.).

The candidate's performance in the two role-plays is assessed against linguistic criteria and clinical communication criteria:

Linguistic Criteria (6 marks each)

1. Intelligibility
2. Fluency
3. Appropriateness
4. Resources of Grammar and Expression

Clinical Communication Criteria (3 marks each)

1. Relationship building
2. Understanding and incorporating the patient's perspective
3. Providing structure
4. Information gathering
5. Information giving

Linguistic criteria

NOTE: The following extracts are examples only. Assessors are carefully trained to assess candidates' sustained performance across both role-plays.

1. Intelligibility

This criterion assesses how well a candidate's speech can be heard and understood. It concerns the impact of such features of speech as pronunciation, rhythm, stress, intonation, pitch and accent on the listener.

Assessors will use this criterion to evaluate the candidate's production of comprehensible speech.

A strong proficiency candidate will:

» use natural flow of speech, giving stress to particular words within sentences to emphasise meaning, e.g., 'I'm unable to do THOSE tests in THIS clinic'.

» use natural flow of speech, giving correct stress to syllables within words so that they are identifiable to the listener, e.g., 'I will reCORD your results'. 'This is an accurate REcord of your results'.

» show control of intonation (voice falling or rising) and stress (appropriate force, length, emphasis or loudness) to enhance meaning and strengthen the communication he/she is wanting to provide.

» pronounce words clearly, for example:
   1. consonants at the end of words or syllables (e.g., 'head', 'weakness').
   2. consonants that distinguish different meanings of similar words (e.g., 'worry', 'worries', 'worried').
   3. consonant sounds at the beginning of words (e.g., /v/ as in '**v**omit', /b/ '**b**ill' versus /p/ '**p**ill').
   4. syllables within words (e.g., 'dang(er)ous', 'a coup(le) of days').
   5. clear initial consonant blends 'problem', 'bleeding'.
   6. word stress in longer words (e.g., 'PAINkiller' not 'painKILLer', 'HOSpital' not 'hosPItal').
   7. vowel sounds (/əʊ/ 'n**o**te' versus /ɒ/ 'n**o**t').

» minimise any intrusive sounds, rhythm and accent which may be influenced by his/her mother tongue.

» show the ability to link words together naturally. For example, there are often no 'spaces' between words in phrases like, 'in_about_an_hour'.

MEDICINE

Now, look at the following examples. Examples 1 and 2 demonstrate HIGH and LOW performances respectively. Some key points are highlighted in each example in relation to the criterion: Intelligibility.

Example 1 — HIGHER

> ... I **think** you can **find**_a few friends who **regularly** go for_a_walk; ↘ you can **start** with_them. ↘ And if_you **reduce** smoking and cut_the amount of **coffee** you drink_a_**day**, it would **help**_your **blood** pressure level. ↘ **Start**_to drink more **water** and do some **exercise**, your **blood** pressure will be **better** in_a month. ↘

Comment

Prosodic features (stress, intonation ↘ and rhythm) are used efficiently. The speech is easily understood even though the evidence of the first language is present. Certain words are linked_together naturally.

Example 2 — LOWER

Wrong		Correct
in**ju**ry	=>	**in**jury
severe	=>	se**ve**re
in**flu**ence	=>	**in**fluence

Comment

Issues with non-standard word level stress and incorrectly pronounced vowels interfere with the listener's ability to understand all information. This affects 'Intelligibility'.

> - ... er... she injured her spine (pronounced as 'spʌn')... is a very important... organ...
>   [sp/aɪ/n]
> - .. may be several months, she can't mobilise (pronounced as 'mobju:laiz') herself...
>   [moub/ə /laiz]

Comment

Vowels are not pronounced correctly, which confuses the patient. The vowel sound in 'spine' [sp/aɪ/n] is not the same as the vowel in 'spun' [sp/ʌ /n], but should be pronounced as [sp/aɪ/n]. The vowel sound in 'mobilise' [moubəlaiz] is not the same as the vowel in 'bureaucrat' [bju:rəkræt], but should be pronounced as [moubəlaiz].

2. Fluency

This criterion assesses how well a candidate's speech is delivered in terms of rate and flow of speech.

Assessors will use this criterion to evaluate the degree to which a candidate is able to speak continuously, evenly and smoothly – without excessive hesitation, repetition, self-correction or use of 'fillers'.

A strong proficiency candidate will:

- maintain a natural speed to make it easier for the listener to follow the message (not too slow, not too fast).
- use even speech (not broken up into fragments) and limit hesitations or speaking in 'bursts' of language.
- avoid overusing sounds (e.g., 'err', 'um', 'ah') and words (e.g., 'OK', 'yes') to fill in gaps.
- use a smoother flow of speech, stressing syllables appropriately and linking words/syllables together.
- use pauses appropriately, for example:
    1. to make his/her meaning clear, e.g., for emphasis.
    2. to separate clearly the points he/she is making.
    3. to think about what he/she is going to say next.
- avoid restarting sentences or repeating words and phrases as he/she corrects himself/herself.

MEDICINE

Look at the following examples. Examples 1 and 2 demonstrate HIGH and LOW performances respectively. Some key points are described on each example in relation to the criterion: Fluency.

Example 1

> "... I think you can find a few friends who regularly go for a walk; you can start with them...(omission)... .
> Start to drink more water and do some exercise, your blood pressure will be better in a month."

Comment

The flow of the speech is good, not too fast or not too slow.

The speech is even and hesitation is rarely evident.

There is little use of 'fillers' (e.g., 'err', 'um', 'OK', etc.).

Restarting sentences is rare.

Example 2

- That is a common concerned from some patients...because they don't know any...don't know more... don't know many medications...something like that...

- You can also give her some... ~~give~~ [let] her inhaler some steams...she can inhaler the steam... That can make her ~~to breath~~ [breathe] easily...

Comment

There is some hesitation that affects fluency.

This candidate often pauses during his/her speech while he/she prepares what to say next.

This 'breaking up' of the message can affect the listener trying to decode it. This affects 'Fluency'.

How to improve

Try to work on a smoother delivery without so many false starts and reformations.

3. Appropriateness

This criterion assesses how well a candidate uses language, register and tone that are appropriate to the situation and the patient.

Assessors will use this criterion to evaluate the degree to which the individual words, grammar and style of speech the candidate selects are appropriate to the particular situation and context.

A strong proficiency candidate will:

» use suitable, professional language.
» use appropriate paraphrasing and re-wording if necessary to explain, in simple terms, technical procedures or medical conditions to a patient who may have little knowledge of these.
» adapt their style and tone to suit the particular situation of the role-play, e.g., giving bad news versus giving positive news or using language suitable for talking to an older person versus a younger person.
» respond appropriately to what the 'patient' says during the role-plays, e.g., the candidate's responses are logically linked with the patient's questions or concerns.
» use language that might reflect the professionalism a health practitioner might require when dealing with patients, e.g., not overly-familiar or informal.
» demonstrate that he/she has the language skills to deal well with complicated situations, e.g., complaints, difficult patients, patients who need convincing, etc.
» use appropriate phrases that are suited to common functions found in medical exchanges, e.g., to 'reassure', 'encourage', 'be supportive', 'explain', etc.
» show awareness of the patient's sensitivities to the condition or information the candidate gives.

MEDICINE

Now, look at the following examples. Examples 1 and 2 demonstrate HIGH and LOW performances respectively. Some key points are described on each example in relation to the criterion: Appropriateness.

Example 1 — HIGHER

> "... What do you think is easier or better for you? Where do you want to start? Do you want to start with ... your eating habit?"

> "... and you do not need to do some intensive fitness activities. I think it's enough if you start with walking for half an hour everyday."

Comment

This candidate uses a good strategy to convince the unwilling patient (e.g., using questions rather than imperative forms to encourage the patient).

An appropriate tone is used to encourage the patient.

Example 2 — LOWER

> - If...she doesn't get treatment ~~effectively~~ *effective*... it may ~~be worsen~~ *get worse*...
> - <u>As far as we know</u>, the antibiotic ~~doesn't~~ *is not* really helpful for viral infections...

Comment

The misuse of natural phrases and expressions is affecting 'Appropriateness'. The underlined phrase indicates considerable doubt, whereas antibiotics definitely do not work for viral infections.

> - If you don't keep *an* eye on this disease...you might ~~get~~ *go* blind unfortunately. But if you keep ~~to do~~ *checking* your blood sugar level and to keep *an* eye on *your* diet...

Comment

At times the message is interrupted by word choice errors. This affects 'Appropriateness'.

How to improve

Take care with phrases that can be easily confused. Meaning breaks down if the phrase is only partially correct.

4. Resources of grammar and expression

This criterion assesses the level and extent of the candidate's grammar and vocabulary resources and their appropriate use.

Assessors will use this criterion to evaluate the range and accuracy of the language resources the candidate has applied in the performance to convey clear meaning.

A strong proficiency candidate will:

- » use appropriate structures to make what he/she is saying coherent, for example, outlining options or choices to a patient (e.g., 'There are several options you can consider. Firstly, in the short term, …').
- » show flexibility by using different phrases to communicate the same idea, if necessary, to make it clearer.
- » form questions correctly, particularly those questions that are often used in health professional/patient dialogues (e.g., 'How long have you been experiencing this?', 'When did the symptoms start?').
- » minimise grammatical inaccuracy to enhance communicative effectiveness.
- » use more complex structures and expressions confidently (e.g., idiomatic speech, sentences with multiple clauses, etc.), i.e., not just a series of simple utterances.
- » use a wide variety of grammatical structures and vocabulary that reflects the depth and range of their linguistic resources.
- » show accurate control of grammatical features including, for example:
  1. correct word order (e.g., 'She broke her tooth' not 'She tooth her broke').
  2. correct use of pronouns/relative pronouns (e.g., 'Tell her it's ok if she (not he) waits then comes back to see me when she (not he) feels better').
  3. correct word choice (e.g., 'Your daughter is breathing more rapidly/repeatedly/regularly' (all have different meanings)).
  4. not omitting words that could affect clear meaning (e.g., 'I recommend that you consider several options including crown, fillings and inlays' not 'I recommend about crown, filling, inlay').
  5. correct use of prepositions (e.g., 'I can explain to you about asthma' not 'I can explain you about asthma').
  6. correct use of articles (e.g., 'A form is completed and then given to the Pharmacist' not 'Form is completed and then given to Pharmacist').
  7. use correct word form (e.g., 'Smoking is dangerous for your health' not 'Smoking is danger for your health').
  8. correct use of countable and uncountable expressions (e.g., 'not many side effects' not 'not much side effects').
  9. use appropriate structures to convey information about time and the sequence of past or future events (e.g., 'We have X-rayed your arm and the results will be available today/next week' not 'We X-ray your arm and the results available').

MEDICINE

Now, look at the following examples. Examples 1 and 2 demonstrate HIGH and LOW performances respectively. Some key points are described on each example in relation to the criterion: Resources of Grammar and Expression.

Example 1

> "... You have two options. The first option is, you're going to have medication, which would be the last solution. The second option, the better option I think, is changing your lifestyle. You do not need to change everything in your life, but you need to make it better..."

Comment

The available options for the patient are outlined in a coherent manner (e.g., 'You have two options. First...').

The number of errors are not intrusive.

Information is given in a confident manner.

Different structures are used to communicate the same idea effectively (e.g., '...is changing your lifestyle. You do not need to change everything...').

Example 2

> - No, I'm not forcing, this is option... *[you]* *[an]*
> - If you have some pain, try not to use too much because I will put some dressing...' *[it]* *[on it]*

Comment

Many sentences are incomplete. Watch out for pronouns such as 'you', 'it' and prepositions such as 'put something on (something)'.

> You need to be free of infections. What you can do is to take some cleaning gloves every time and <u>do something</u> with clean clothes <u>and something like that</u>...

Comment

Many simple words are used repetitively, affecting "Resources of Grammar and Expression'. In the above example, 'something' is overused, indicating gaps in vocabulary.

How to improve
Be more specific with word choice.

OET Speaking clinical communication criteria

A: Indicators of relationship building		
A1	Initiating the interaction appropriately (greeting, introductions)	Initiating the interview appropriately helps establish rapport and a supportive environment. Initiation involves greeting the patient, introducing yourself, clarifying the patient's name and clarifying your role in their care. The nature of the interview can be explained and if necessary negotiated.
A2	Demonstrating an attentive and respectful attitude	Throughout the interview, demonstrating attentiveness and respect establishes trust with the patient, lays down the foundation for a collaborative relationship and ensures that the patient understands your motivation to help. Examples of such behaviour would include attending to the patient's comfort, asking permission and consent to proceed, and being sensitive to potentially embarrassing or distressing matters.
A3	Demonstrating a non-judgemental approach	Accepting the patient's perspective and views reassuringly and non-judgementally without initial rebuttal is a key component of relationship building. A judgemental response to patients' ideas and concerns devalues their contributions. A non-judgemental response would include accepting the patient's perspective and acknowledging the legitimacy of the patient to hold their own views and feelings.
A4	Showing empathy for feelings/ predicament/ emotional state	Empathy is one of the key skills of building the relationship. Empathy involves the understanding and sensitive appreciation of another person's predicament or feelings and the communication of that understanding back to the patient in a supportive way. This can be achieved through both non-verbal and verbal behaviours. Even with audio alone, some non-verbal behaviours such as the use of silence and appropriate voice tone in response to a patient's expression of feelings can be observed. Verbal empathy makes this more explicit by specifically naming and appreciating the patient's emotions or predicament.

MEDICINE

B: Indicators of understanding and incorporating the patient's perspective

B1	Eliciting and exploring patient's ideas/concerns/expectations	Understanding the patient's perspective is a key component of patient-centred health care. Each patient has a unique experience of sickness that includes the feelings, thoughts, concerns and effect on life that any episode of sickness induces. Patients may either volunteer this spontaneously (as direct statements or cues) or in response to health professionals' enquiries.
B2	Picking up patient's cues	Patients are generally eager to tell us about their own thoughts and feelings but often do so indirectly through verbal hints or changes in non-verbal behaviour (such as vocal cues including hesitation or change in volume). Picking up these cues is essential for exploring both the biomedical and the patient's perspectives. Some of the techniques for picking up cues would include echoing, i.e. repeating back what has just been said and either adding emphasis where appropriate or turning the echoed statement into a question, e.g. *"Something could be done…?"*. Another possibility is more overtly checking out statements or hints, e.g. *"I sense that you are not happy with the explanations you've been given in the past"*
B3	Relating explanations to elicited ideas/concerns/expectations	One of the key reasons for discovering the patient's perspective is to incorporate this into explanations often in the later aspects of the interview. If the explanation does not address the patient's individual ideas, concerns and expectations, then recall, understanding and satisfaction suffer as the patient is still worrying about their still unaddressed concerns

C: Indicators of providing structure

C1	Sequencing the interview purposefully and logically	It is the responsibility of the health professional to maintain a logical sequence apparent to the patient as the interview unfolds. An ordered approach to organisation helps both professional and patient in efficient and accurate data gathering and information-giving. This needs to be balanced with the need to be patient-centred and follow the patient's needs. Flexibility and logical sequencing need to be thoughtfully combined. It is more obvious when sequencing is inadequate: the health professional will meander aimlessly or jump around between segments of the interview making the patient unclear as to the point of specific lines of enquiry.
C2	Signposting changes in topic	Signposting is a key skill in enabling patients to understand the structure of the interview by making the organisation overt: not only the health professional but also the patient needs to understand where the interview is going and why. A signposting statement introduces and draws attention to what we are about to say. For instance, it is helpful to use a signposting statement to introduce a summary. Signposting can also be used to make the progression from one section to another and explain the rationale for the next section.
C3	Using organising techniques in explanations	A variety of skills help to organise explanations in a way that leads particularly to increased patient recall and understanding. Skills include: categorisation in which the health professional informs the patient about which categories of information are to be provided labelling in which important points are explicitly labelled by the health professional. This can be achieved by using emphatic phrases or adverb intensifiers chunking in which information is delivered in chunks with clear gaps in between sections before proceeding repetition and summary of important points

MEDICINE

D: Indicators for information-gathering

D1	Facilitating patient's narrative with active listening techniques, minimising interruption	Listening to the patient's narrative, particularly at the beginning of an interview, enables the health professional to more efficiently discover the story, hear the patient's perspective, appear supportive and interested and pick up cues to patients' feelings. Interruption of the narrative has the opposite effect and in particular generally leads to a predominantly biomedical history, omitting the patient's perspective. Observable skills of active listening techniques include: **A.** the use of silence and pausing **B.** verbal encouragement such as *um, uh-huh, I see* **C.** echoing and repetition such as "*chest pain?*" or "*not coping?*" **D.** paraphrasing and interpretation such as "*Are you thinking that when John gets even more ill, you won't be strong enough to nurse him at home by yourself?*"
D2	Using initially open questions, appropriately moving to closed questions	Understanding how to intentionally choose between open and closed questioning styles at different points in the interview is of key importance. An effective health professional uses open questioning techniques first to obtain a picture of the problem from the patient's perspective. Later, the approach becomes more focused with increasingly specific though still open questions and eventually closed questions to elicit additional details that the patient may have omitted. The use of open questioning techniques is critical at the beginning of the exploration of any problem and the most common mistake is to move to closed questioning too quickly. Closed questions are questions for which a specific and often one word answer is elicited. These responses are often "*yes/no*". *Open questioning techniques* in contrast are designed to introduce an area of enquiry without unduly shaping or focusing the content of the response. They still direct the patient to a specific area but allow the patient more discretion in their answer, suggesting to the patient that elaboration is both appropriate and welcome.
D3	NOT using compound questions/ leading questions	A compound question is when more than one question is asked without allowing time to answer. It confuses the patient about what information is wanted, and introduces uncertainty about which of the questions asked the eventual reply relates to. An example would be "*have you ever had chest pain or felt short of breath?*" A leading question includes an assumption in the question which makes it more difficult for the respondent to contradict the assumption. e.g., "*You've lost weight, haven't you?* or "*you haven't had any ankle swelling?*"

D4	Clarifying statements which are vague or need amplification	Clarifying statements which are vague or need further amplification is a vital information gathering skill. After an initial response to an open ended question, health professionals may need to prompt patients for more precision, clarity or completeness. Often patients' statements can have two (or more) possible meanings: it is important to ascertain which one is intended.
D5	Summarising information to encourage correction/ invite further information	Summarising is the deliberate step of making an explicit verbal summary to the patient of the information gathered so far and is one of the most important of all information gathering skills. Used periodically throughout the interview, it helps with two significant tasks – ensuring accuracy and facilitating the patient's further responses.

E: Indicators for information-giving

E1	Establishing initially what patient already knows	One key interactive approach to giving information to patients involves assessing their prior knowledge. This allows you to determine at what level to pitch information, how much and what information the patient needs, and the degree to which your view of the problem differs from that of the patient.
E2	Pausing periodically when giving information, using response to guide next steps	This approach, often called chunking and checking, is a vital skill throughout the information-giving phase of the interview. Here, the health professional gives information in small pieces, pausing and checking for understanding before proceeding and being guided by the patient's reactions to see what information is required next. This technique is a vital component of assessing the patient's overall information needs: if you give information in small chunks and give patients ample opportunity to contribute, they will respond with clear signals about both the amount and type of information they still require.
E3	Encouraging patient to contribute reactions/feelings	A further element of effective information giving is providing opportunities to the patient to ask questions, seek clarification or express doubts. Health professionals have to be very explicit here: many patients are reluctant to express what is on the tip of their tongue and are extremely hesitant to ask the doctor questions. Unless positively invited to do so, they may leave the consultation with their questions unanswered and a reduced understanding and commitment to plans.
E4	Checking whether patient has understood information	Checking the patient has understood the information given is an important step in ensuring accuracy of information transfer. This can be done by asking "*does that make sense?*" although many patients will say yes when they mean no to avoid looking stupid. A more effective method is to use patient restatement, i.e. asking the patient to repeat back to the doctor what has been discussed to ensure that their understanding is the same
E5	Discovering what further information patient needs	Deliberately asking the patient what other information would be helpful enables the health professional to directly discover areas to address which the health professional might not have considered. It is difficult to guess each patient's individual needs and asking directly is an obvious way to prevent the omission of important information.

Useful language

Greeting / Introduction

- Good morning/afternoon/evening.
- Nice to see you (again).
- How are you today?
- My name is Dr .../I'm Dr ...
- Thanks for coming to see me today.
- Pleased to meet you (response to patient's introduction).

Getting information

Starting the interview:
- What brings you along here today?
- What brought you here today?
- What seems to be the trouble/problem?
- How can I help you?
- What can I do for you?
- What seems to be bothering you?

Asking about location of the problem:
- Where is the sensation?
- Can you tell me where it hurts?
- Where do you feel sore?
- Where does it feel sore?
- Which part of the/your body is affected?
- Show me where the pain is.
- Tell me where the pain is.

Asking about duration:
- When did it start?
- How long have you had it?
- How long have you been feeling like this?
- How often has this been occurring?
- How long have you been suffering from this problem?
- When did the problem start?

Asking about severity of pain or type of pain:
- Is the pain dull or sharp?
- What is the pain like?
- Could you describe the pain?
- How severe is the pain?
- Does it disturb you at night?
- Does it feel numb?
- Does it occur all of the time or just now and again?

Questioning

To clarify/to get details:
- Have you had any...?
- Does the discomfort appear to be brought on by anything in particular?
- What do you do when you get the pain?
- Do you ever get pain at night?
- Does anything special make it worse?
- Does anything seem to bring it on/aggravate the problem?
- Is there anything that seems to relieve this?

MEDICINE

Prescribing

Tests, medicine, treatment:
- I think we would start with…
- I will give you a prescription for…
- I will give you a referral for…
- I'll write a referral letter to…
- I'm going to ask you to fill a prescription for…
- We'll run some tests to see…

Check understanding
- Do you have any questions?
- Have you ever heard of …?

Reassurance
- I can understand your concerns, but…
- I'm sure you won't have any more trouble…
- Don't worry, it'll go away by itself/in a few days/with some rest…
- Rest assured, this is quite common…
- There is nothing to be overly concerned about.

Feedback
Respond to patient's questions:
- Were there any other questions?
- Does this sound ok/like an acceptable plan?

Advising / Suggesting
- What I think we'll do is …
- What I suggest you do is …
- It is worthwhile…
- I advise you…
- We could make a time to follow up on that.
- It's a good idea to …

Leave-taking

Pleasure to meet you.
- Nice to meet you, …
- Let's leave it there.
- All the best, …
- I'll see you next time/soon.
- Thanks very much for coming to see me.

Notes

Printed in Poland
by Amazon Fulfillment
Poland Sp. z o.o., Wrocław